LETTER TO A FRIEND

Nagarjuna's Classic Text

Books by Traleg Kyabgon

Integral Buddhism: Developing All Aspects of One's Personhood, Shogam Publications, 2018

King Doha: Saraha's Advice to a King, Shogam Publications, 2018

Song of Karmapa: The Aspiration of the Mahamudra of True Meaning by Lord Rangjung Dorje, Shogam Publications, 2018

Moonbeams of Mahamudra: The Classic Meditation Manual, Shogam Publications, 2015

Karma: What it is, What it isn't, and Why it matters, Shambhala Publications, 2015

Four Dharmas of Gampopa, KTD Publications, 2013

Asanga's Abhidharmasamuccaya, KTD Publications, 2013

Ninth Karmapa Wangchuk Dorje's Ocean Of Certainty, KTD Publications, 2011

Influence of Yogacara on Mahamudra, KTD Publications, 2010

The Practice of Lojong: Cultivating Compassion through Training the Mind, Shambhala Publications, 2007

Mind at Ease: Self-Liberation through Mahamudra Meditation, Shambhala Publications, 2004

Benevolent Mind: A Manual in Mind Training, Zhisil Chokyi Ghatsal, 2003

The Essence of Buddhism: An Introduction to Its Philosophy and Practice, Shambhala Publications, 2002 & 2014

Photo facing page: Traleg Kyabgon Rinpoche the Ninth

LETTER TO A FRIEND

Nagarjuna's Classic Text

Translation and Oral Commentary

Traleg Kyabgon

Foreword by Khenchen Thrangu Rinpoche

SHOGAM
PUBLICATIONS
2018

Shogam Publications Pty Ltd
PO Box 239 Ballarat, Victoria, Australia, 3353
www.shogam.org
info@shogam.com

First Edition

Printed in Australia and the United States of America

Edited by Virginia Golding

Designed by David Bennett

National Library of Australia
Kyabgon, Traleg, 1955
Letter to a Friend: Nagarjuna's Classic Text

Printed book ISBN: 978-0-6481148-2-6 (paperback)
E-book ISBN: 978-0-6481148-3-3

DEDICATION

For Traleg Kyabgon Rinpoche

Thank you for illuminating the dark
with the vastness of your being

Contents

Foreword

Nagarjuna's *Letter to a Friend* is one of the best loved Buddhist texts. It gives advice applying to everyone, whether householders or monastics, on how to live one's life in the world and also to practice the dharma. Nagarjuna wrote this as a letter in verse to his friend and patron King Gautamiputra, a wealthy and powerful individual who had great merit and faith in the dharma as well as the many responsibilities that come with power and influence. This letter gave him many instructions on how to inspire himself to practice the dharma in his own busy and distracting position, counsel that is still pertinent to people in the developed societies of our modern era. Just as King Gautamiputra needed to find a way to incorporate dharma practice into his own opulent but busy lifestyle, people in this day and age often have great demands of work and family that they need to fulfill at the same time as they practice the dharma. These verses provide instructions in easy-to-understand verse that clearly communicate how we can bring genuine practice of the dharma into our lives.

It is also especially helpful for Nagarjuna's classic text to be accompanied by an explanation by the Ninth Traleg Kyabgon Rinpoche. The Traleg Kyabgon first received a thorough education in the traditional Buddhist canon before moving to Australia, where he studied Western Philosophy. He spent many decades in Australia and Western countries, developing a thorough command of English as well as a deep understanding of Western students' backgrounds. He thus became highly skilled in communicating with them in ways that were easy for them to understand. For this reason, pairing this translation of Nagarjuna's classic text with Traleg Kyabgon's explanation will be especially beneficial for English-language readers. We are all fortunate indeed to read this priceless advice from Nagarjuna and Traleg Kyabgon.

Khenchen Thrangu Rinpoche the Ninth
Namo Buddha
Thrangu Tashi Yangtse Monastery
Nepal 2018

Biography of Author

TRALEG KYABGON RINPOCHE IX

Traleg Kyabgon Rinpoche IX (1955-2012) was born in Nangchen in Kham, eastern Tibet. He was recognized by His Holiness XVI Gyalwang Karmapa as the ninth Traleg tulku and enthroned at the age of two as the supreme abbot of Thrangu Monastery. Rinpoche was taken to Rumtek Monastery in Sikkim at the age of four where he was educated with other young tulkus in exile by His Holiness Karmapa for the next five years.

Rinpoche began his studies under the auspices of His Eminence Kyabje Thuksey Rinpoche at Sangngak Choling in Darjeeling. He also studied with a number of other eminent Tibetan teachers during that time and mastered the many Tibetan teachings with the Kagyu and Nyingma traditions in particular including the *Havajra Tantra*, *Guhyasamaja Tantra*, and the third Karmapa's *Zabmo Nangdon* (*The Profound Inner Meaning*) under Khenpo Noryang (abbot of Sangngak Choling). Rinpoche studied the Abhidharmakosha, Pramanavarttika, Bodhisattvacharyavatara, *Abhidharmasamuccaya*, *Six Treaties of Nagarjuna*, the *Madhyanta-vibhaga*, and the *Mahayanuttaratantra* with Khenpo Sogyal. He also studied with Khenpo Sodar and was trained in tantric ritual practices by Lama Ganga, who had been specifically sent by His Holiness Karmapa for that purpose.

In 1967 Rinpoche moved to the Institute of Higher Tibetan Studies in Sarnath, and studied extensively for the next five years.

He studied Buddhist history, Sanskrit, and Hindi, as well as Longchenpa's *Finding Comfort and Ease* (*Ngalso Korsum*), *Seven Treasuries* (*Longchen Dzod Dun*), *Three Cycles of Liberation* (*Rangdrol Korsum*), and *Longchen Nyingthig* with Khenchen Palden Sherab Rinpoche and Khenpo Tsondru.

When Rinpoche had completed these studies at the age of sixteen, he was sent by His Holiness Karmapa to study under the auspices of the Venerable Khenpo Yesha Chodar at Sanskrit University in Varanasi for three years. Rinpoche was also tutored by khenpos and geshes from all four traditions of Tibetan Buddhism during this time.

Rinpoche was subsequently put in charge of Zangdog Palri Monastery (the glorious copper colored mountain) in Eastern Bhutan and placed under the private tutelage of Dregung Khenpo Ngedon by His Holiness Karmapa to continue his studies of Sutra and Tantra. He ran this monastery for the next three years and began learning English during this time.

From 1977 to 1980, Rinpoche returned to Rumtek in Sikkim to fill the honored position of His Holiness' translator, where he dealt with many English-speaking Western visitors.

Rinpoche moved to Melbourne, Australia in 1980 and commenced studies in comparative religion and philosophy at LaTrobe University. Rinpoche established E-Vam Institute in Melbourne in 1982 and went on to establish further Centers in Australia, America, and New Zealand. For the next 25 years Rinpoche gave weekly teachings, intensive weekend courses, and retreats on classic Kagyu and Nyingma texts. During this time Rinpoche also taught internationally travelling extensively through America, Europe, and South East Asia and was appointed the Spiritual Director of Kamalashila Institute in Germany for five years in the 1980's.

Rinpoche established a retreat center, Maitripa Centre in

Healesville, Australia in 1997 where he conducted two public retreats a year. Rinpoche founded E-Vam Buddhist Institute in the U.S in 2000, and Nyima Tashi Buddhist Centre in New Zealand 2004. In 2010 Rinpoche established a Buddhist college called Shogam Vidhalaya at E-Vam Institute in Australia and instructed students on a weekly basis.

Throughout his life Rinpoche gave extensive teachings on many aspects of Buddhist psychology and philosophy, as well as comparative religion, and Buddhist and Western thought. He was an active writer and has many titles to his name. Titles include: the best selling *Essence of Buddhism*; *Karma, What It Is, What It Isn't, and Why It Matters*; *The Practice of Lojong*; *Moonbeams of Mahamudra*; and many more. Many of Rinpoche's books are translated in to a number of different languages including Chinese, French, German, Korean and Spanish. Rinpoche's writings are thought provoking, challenging, profound, and highly relevant to today's world and its many challenges.

Rinpoche was active in publishing during the last two decades of his life, beginning with his quarterly magazine Ordinary Mind which ran from 1997 to 2003. Further, Rinpoche founded his own publishing arm Shogam Publications in 2008 and released a number of books on Buddhist history, philosophy, and psychology and left instructions for the continuation of this vision. His vision for Shogam and list of titles can be found at www.shogam.com.

Rinpoche's ecumenical approach can be seen in his other activities aimed at bringing buddhadharma to the West. He established the biannual Buddhism and Psychotherapy Conference (1994 - 2003), and Tibet Here and Now Conference (2005), and the annual Buddhist Summer School (1984 to the present).

Traleg Kyabgon Rinpoche IX passed into parinirvana on 24 July 2012, on Chokhor Duchen, the auspicious day of the Buddha's first teaching. Rinpoche stayed in meditation (*thugdam*) for weeks after his passing. A traditional cremation ceremony was conducted at Maitripa Centre and a stupa was erected on the center's grounds in Rinpoche's honor.

It is a privilege to continue to release the profound teachings of Traleg Kyabgon Rinpoche IX given in the West for over 30 years. Rinpoche's Sangha hope that many will benefit.

Acknowledgements

Thanks to everyone on the Shogam team who helped me so much. As editor, my role was limited in comparison to others who contributed to this book and who are committed to sharing Traleg Kyabgon Rinpoche's precious and beautiful teachings. Claire Blaxell for her time, for her fantastic transcripts, amazing attention to detail, and very helpful suggestions. Felicity Lodro for her dedication to sharing Traleg Kyabgon's wisdom more broadly and without whom this book would not be, along with her organizational talents, support, and all of her additional contributions to the book, of which there are many. Salvatore Celiento for his keen editorial eyes, suggestions, and the gift of his time, and David Bennett for his beautiful book design and his unique talents in this area. Lastly, to my husband Steve who always said the right things at the right time.

Virginia Golding

Editor's Introduction

In almost all schools of Mahayana Buddhism, the great Indian master Arya Nagarjuna is considered one of the most important scholars of this tradition (Kalupahana 1986). Nagarjuna is also recognized as one of the greatest philosophers in Asian history, although contemporary scholars know very little detail about his life. It is not clear when he lived, although it is proposed it was somewhere between the 1st and 3rd centuries AD (Westerhoff 2009). In his oral commentary on "*The Collection of Middle Way Reasoning*," Khen Rinpoche Namdrol (Rinpoche n.d.) states that Nagarjuna was prophesied by the Buddha himself in the "*Root Tantra of Manjusuri*" (*Manjusrimula Tantra*) and was to be born four hundred years after the Buddha's own parinirvana and live for six hundred years.

Much of what is known of Nagarjuna has been passed down mostly in the form of legend. What is evident is that he was a monk and the principal Abbot of Nalanda, a large and renowned Buddhist monastery in the ancient kingdom of Guptas or modern-day Bihar, nearby the town of Rajgir in India. Nalanda was first established in the 5th century BC and it is understood the Buddha himself visited the monastery. Nalanda came to be known as a place of great learning during the period in which Nagarjuna resided as Abbot and it was largely due to him that Nalanda's reputation was established. Nagarjuna is also known for his remarkable ability to summarize and condense the Buddha's vast teachings, along with his extraordinary capacity to expound their profound meaning (Group 2005).

Nagarjuna was also a prolific writer, with over 116 different texts in the Tibetan Canon attributed to him, which vary enormously in their diversity (Westerhoff 2009). These texts include several commentaries on sutra and tantra, which demonstrates that he was practicing both (Karmapa 2009). Nagarjuna addressed his works to a wide audience despite being a monastic and Abbot of Nalanda. The overriding theme in Nagarjuna's work considers the way in which a bodhisattva (a person wishing to attain the state of Buddhahood) may travel the path to enlightenment and the merit and wisdom one needs to cultivate to achieve this goal. According to Nagarjuna, wisdom or prajna is the Perfection of Wisdom, which is the knowledge of emptiness or dependent origination (*pratityasamutpada*). Nagarjuna is credited with transforming the Buddha's teachings in Perfection of Wisdom sutras (*prajnaparamita*) into the philosophical system of Madhyamaka. The doctrine of emptiness is a central theme of the Madhyamaka philosophical school and therefore sits within the tradition associated with the Perfection of Wisdom literature of Mahayana Buddhism (Lopez 1998).

It is Nagarjuna's text entitled the "*Root Verses on the Middle Way*" (*Mulamadhyamakakaraka*) that provided the basis from which the entire Madhyamaka is founded. His Holiness the 17th Karmapa (Karmapa 2009), states that there are two accounts of how Nagarjuna came to write this text. The first tells of how the King of the Nagas (water spirits) gave these books to Nagarjuna. The other is from a biography of Nagarjuna written by the great Indian scholar Kumarajiva, who is said to have translated many Buddhist texts into Chinese. Kumarajiva states that Nagarjuna had a vision in which he entered a jeweled palace where he met a great bodhisattva who showed him many caskets containing sutras. According to the Kumarajiva, when Nagarjuna rose from this vision he then wrote down what he had read, which was the

100,000 Stanza Perfection of Wisdom Sutra.

Another of Nagarjuna's famous and seminal texts is the "*Letter to a Friend*" or *Suhrillekha* (Sanskrit). Traleg Kyabgon Rinpoche IX (1955-2012) very kindly provided commentary to this text in a series of teachings given at the Maitripa Contemplative Centre in Healesville, Australia and these teachings are the subject of this book. Rinpoche translated directly from an Indian commentary written in Sanskrit by Aryadeva, a student of Nagarjuna as well as referred to a translation of the verses and commentary by Ven. Lozang Jamspal, Ven. Ngawang Samten Chophel, and Peter Della Santina. According to His Holiness 17th Karmapa, Nagarjuna's Letter was composed mainly as an instruction for householders on how to practice dharma (Karmapa 2009). Nagarjuna's Letter was written to his friend the King Gautamiputra who is believed to have lived in the south of India in the modern state of Andhra Pradesh, although unfortunately very little is known of the King's life.

Nagarjuna's "*Letter to a Friend*" provides a condensed and concise summary of the Mahayana path in only 123 verses. As such, it is not easily accessible to most audiences without a good understanding of the Buddha's original sutras. Works like the Letter were written in the form of verses so that they could be more easily memorized by those wishing to study the Dharma. As the Letter explores various subjects taught by the Buddha, Tibetan authors wishing to explain certain points of Buddhist philosophy could quote them as convenient sources of scripture (Group 2005). Nagarjuna's "*Letter to a Friend*" offers advice on many subjects for those wishing to follow the Mahayana path. For example, Nagarjuna offers practical instruction regarding how to conduct one's individual life and relationships with others, covering subjects such as virtue, discipline, morality, and filial relations, proceeding onto the profound teachings regarding the relative and ultimate truths.

According to Traleg Rinpoche, the principal theme of

Nagarjuna's Letter is the teaching on the *six reminders*: the Buddha, Dharma, and Sangha, referring to Buddha Shakyamuni, his teachings, and those who follow his teachings, as well as the practice of generosity, moral precepts, and the qualities of gods. With regards to the last reminder, Rinpoche states that Nagarjuna is referring to cultivating one's mind, particularly in terms of the refinement one's mental states, which is achieved through the practice of samadhi or meditative concentration.

Common to many Indian texts of his period, Nagarjuna begins his Letter with a commitment to compose the text, followed by guidance regarding the way to approach the text correctly. Rinpoche states Aryadeva's commentary suggests Nagarjuna is not particularly concerned about the poetic elegance of his composition, but rather the content of his text. Nagarjuna wants to convey that the text is not meant to prove his skill in poetic composition, but rather to convey the teachings of the Buddha effectively. Nagarjuna then discusses the importance of reflecting on the *six reminders* which inspire faith as well giving encouragement, and the importance of the threefold process of hearing or studying, thinking, and meditating. Nagarjuna continues to the main text of the Letter, where Nagarjuna offers the King pragmatic advice by emphasizing a core teaching of the Buddha regarding the importance of practicing the ten virtuous deeds, while also advising him to avoid the ten actions which cause suffering. Traleg Rinpoche's commentary states that it is by "following a livelihood based on refraining from the ten non-virtuous deeds and the cultivation of the ten virtuous deeds that leads to the experience of the coincidence of aspiration and satisfaction of one's desires."

Nagarjuna's practical advice also includes dealing with destructive tendencies in oneself. In order to work constructively with habitual tendencies such as the craving of food, alcohol, gambling, or other behaviors that perpetuate one's suffering, Nagarjuna suggests that laypeople engage in taking moral precepts from time to time. One choses to refrain from certain behaviors that are causing one difficulties for a period of time. Traleg Rinpoche states that "as one begins to practice in this way one can exercise some power or liberty regarding one's actions. Even if one is still enslaved to certain impulses or tendencies or deep-seated habit patterns and may have a hard time giving them up, taking these precepts does cause interruptions in these patterns." Much of the Letter contains guidance on what we can do to bring about some behavioral modification and skillful ways in which to do this.

According to Traleg Rinpoche, Nagarjuna places a strong emphasis in the Letter on self-control and character development and proposes this needs to be done in conjunction with fundamental changes in one's attitudes which keep us in states of suffering. These are attitudes such as miserliness, insincerity, deception, laziness, conceit, haughtiness, excessive attachment to material things, hostility, being proud of one's station in life, of one's physical beauty, of one's education and so on. Rinpoche states that by becoming conscious of these attitudes within oneself and applying the strategy of taking precepts, one can mature and flourish. This also enables the aspiring bodhisattva to more easily engage in meditative practice as one becomes calmer, making the practice of meditation easier to do.

Another core theme of the text is the Buddha's teaching on the *six paramitas*: generosity, moral precepts, patience, vigor or diligence, meditative concentration, and wisdom. According to Traleg Rinpoche, the practice of generosity and moral precepts in the context of the *six paramitas* is different from the way in which moral precepts is discussed earlier in the text. In this context, a Mahayana practitioner practices generosity and moral precepts with *bodhicitta* in mind where *bodhicitta* means "enlightened heart" which is generated by considering the welfare of all sentient beings.

Also included in the Letter is the Buddha's foundational teaching of the noble eightfold path, which encompasses the three disciplines or higher trainings of Morality, Meditation, and Wisdom. Nagarjuna strongly emphasizes the importance of morality and ethics and places the virtue of generosity at their foundation, warning against the consequences of arrogance, greediness, or miserliness. Traleg Rinpoche's commentary states this is because "miserliness, hostility, and haughtiness cause considerable disruption and discontentment in one's life," and that, "learning to be generous is the very foundation of all of one's moral practices." Rinpoche also states Nagarjuna's emphasis on morality makes it clear Nagarjuna is seeking to communicate the importance that living a moral life has in becoming a person of character and depth. In becoming a person of character, Traleg Rinpoche states Nagarjuna highlights the importance of preserving ones "inner wealth" which is accrued by cultivating the Seven Treasures: faith, morality, giving, studying, modesty, humility, and wisdom. One must also be heedful of avoiding the six indulgences, which will result in the loss of these treasures and will diminish an individual's reputation, causing rebirth in lower realms.

According to historical sources, the Seven Noble Treasures were given by the Buddha to his only son Rahula. The story recounts that Rahula's mother the princess Yasodhara persuaded her son to ask his father what his inheritance would be after the Buddha's return to Kapilavastu. When asked this question by his young son, the Buddha offered a profound teaching, pointing out the fragile, impermanent nature of worldly objects where the pursuit of wealth, be it gold, silver, fields, or houses, leads only to suffering. Instead he spoke to Rahula of the value of accruing the Seven Noble Treasures of Faith, Morality, Giving, Study, Modesty, Humility, and Wisdom (Della Santina n.d.). Rinpoche's commentary adds these can be understood as "trust, a sense of ethical standing, generosity, learning, trying to be beyond reproach, having some kind of shame or feeling of embarrassment, and having sensitivity towards others."

Nagarjuna also offers advice concerning the importance of observing basic social values and of harmonious filial relations. Traleg Rinpoche states that Nagarjuna is instructing the reader to consider how to relate to one's parents and family members because having good relationships with one's family and friends reflects the quality of life one will have. Rinpoche states that "the same kind of attitude one may develop with near and dear ones could gradually extend to others, to people who we may have fewer dealings with or people who are not necessarily close or dear to us," and that, "This will then provide a genuine foundation for all of one's relationships with all beings, including those we have very tiring and trying relationships or those we may look up to or seek guidance and counsel from, so we can have tangible results in this life."

Nagarjuna also highlights the importance of choosing one's friends wisely, clarifying his point by using the simile of mangoes. Some he says appear to be ripe, but are not, others appear to be unripe, but are ripe, while others appear to be unripe and are unripe, while others appear to be ripe and are ripe. According to Traleg Rinpoche, "This means that some people may be a bit nasty, but they come across as being very nice and people who are actually quite nice inside, but who come across as being very unpleasant. Some people are unpleasant full stop—both unpleasant inside and unpleasant on the outside—and then there are those who are pleasant both inside and outside." Rinpoche's commentary states that Nagarjuna is emphasizing the importance of having a strong character, otherwise we will be too easily influenced by others. Accordingly, one's choice of friends is an important factor in leading a good life.

Along with advice on managing one's negative behaviors and of refraining from entertaining unwholesome attitudes, Nagarjuna also stresses the importance of cultivating contentment, of having few desires, and of patience or *kshanti*. According to Traleg Rinpoche, "patience means having the courage and fortitude to face difficulties and not expect everything to be smooth sailing." Rinpoche states that it is important to approach Buddhist practice in an integrated way, where all aspects of our being are brought to bear in our effort to gain liberation from samsaric existence. Traleg Rinpoche's commentary notes that Nagarjuna's advice warns of the negative outcomes of not cultivating these capacities and qualities within ourselves, "so that we will be able to keep ourselves from sliding back into what are called lower forms of existence or degraded states where negative emotions are rampant with feelings of dejection, lack of appreciation, and depression."

Having few desires and cultivating a sense of contentment are also a necessary preparation for the practice of meditation. Nagarjuna continues his Letter with guidance on the practice of shamatha or tranquility meditation. In this practice, one cultivates the four levels of concentration or the four states of samadhi, which refer to different levels of meditative attainment. These are described as corresponding to the states of the gods, the first with "Brahma" the second samadhi with "Abhasvara," the third with "Subhakritsna," and the fourth one with "Brihatphala." Nagarjuna goes onto discuss the value of engaging in the *Brahma-vihara* or four immeasurables or practice of loving kindness, compassion, joy, and equanimity as these meditations lead one to experience divine states. Rinpoche's commentary suggests these meditations should be practiced alongside tranquility meditation and offers a rich teaching on how to approach this profound practice while contemplating the relative and ultimate truths.

Nagarjuna also stresses the importance of refraining from

unnecessary speculation on such topics as metaphysics as it only serves as a distraction to the goal of awakening. One needs to stay focused on the task at hand and not be easily led astray. Referring to Nagarjuna's verse concerning the importance of abandoning wrong views and cultivating right view, Rinpoche states that those who follow the Buddhist path have two different kinds of desires in terms of self-fulfillment. The first being a temporary and immediate goal and the second being a more distant, sublime goal. The immediate goal is one of trying to improve and lift ourselves up and to develop and mature while attaining higher and higher states of mind. The more distant goal is to attain enlightenment. Traleg Rinpoche suggests that Nagarjuna's point is that if we have these desires, then we should be doing more than simply engaging in virtuous actions and shamatha or calming meditation, we need to have right view, and this is cultivated though insight or vipashayana meditation.

Nagarjuna's remarkable capacity to be concise while elucidating highly complex concepts is evident throughout the text. In just one verse concerning the nature of the aggregates he highlights the various arguments of the dominant philosophical schools of ancient India concerning the nature of reality. Traleg Rinpoche's commentary demonstrates through the process of negation how these arguments lead to an incorrect view and therefore need to be discarded, but not before they are well understood and meditated upon. Concerning right view, Nagarjuna also articulates in just a few verses the profound teachings of the Buddha on the relative and ultimate truths. For example, verses that expound the four-fold truths, interdependent origination, the four seals and the twelve links of interdependent arising. Nagarjuna's points of advice and statements on profound and subtle ancient Indian and Buddhist philosophy would be inaccessible to many without Traleg Rinpoche's ability to make difficult philosophical arguments more accessible for the reader not well versed in these subjects and attests to his vast knowledge and depth of understanding of Nagarjuna's work and the Buddha's teachings.

Traleg Rinpoche's commentary covers most of the verses in the original letter except for verses related to conditioned existence or the difficulties of living in samsara. This was because Rinpoche was speaking to an audience he believed were already familiar with this topic and commented he thought many of the audience members may have read Patrul Rinpoche's work, "*Words of my Perfect Teacher*." Readers of this commentary unfamiliar with this subject are therefore encouraged to read this text.

In concluding the text, Rinpoche's commentary suggests Nagarjuna is fully aware that what he is suggesting the King do is a great deal, and acknowledges that even an ordained person would find it extremely difficult. The point is that one must do whatever one can. Rinpoche states that, "If we do something often enough there is nothing that does not become easier as our capacity is extended through sheer practice." Through familiarity, whatever the task, it will become easier over time and the King needs to realize this as well.

In providing an overview of many of the main themes covered in Nagarjuna's letter, it is hoped the reader of this text will gain some understanding of the importance and value it has within the Tibetan Buddhist Canon and for those wishing to follow the bodhisattva path of Mahayana Buddhism. It has been a privilege to have edited Traleg Rinpoche's commentary on "*Nagarjuna's Letter to a Friend*" while also a challenge to keep the text true to his style of teaching so that readers can have a feel for not only his brilliance as a scholar but the ease and often conversational style with which he taught. Traleg Rinpoche IX is known not only as a great scholar and teacher, but one who understood how to teach and engage Western students in a way not many Tibetan Buddhist teachers have in the recent past.

Virginia Golding

Editor's Biography

Virginia Golding, BA (Psychology Philosophy), MSW, is a psychotherapist, consultant, and educator. She has been a student and practitioner of Tibetan Buddhism under the guidance of the late Traleg Kyabgon Rinpoche the Ninth for many years. In recent times Virginia has continued her studies of Tibetan Buddhism in Australia and India attending teachings by His Holiness the Seventeenth Karmapa, Yangten Tulku Rinpoche, and Mingyur Rinpoche and spent 3 months studying in Dharamsala with Khenpo Chamtrul Rinpoche. In Australia Virginia works in private practice, regularly teaches at Traleg Rinpoche's Centre, E-Vam Institute in Melbourne, and leads weekend retreats through her private practice.

LETTER TO A FRIEND

Nagarjuna's Classic Text

Introduction to Text

Nagarjuna's[1] "Letter to King Gautamiputra[2]," *Suhrillekha* (Sanskrit) or *Letter to a Friend*, "*she ting*" (*Suhrillekha, pa'i bshes spring yig*) in Tibetan, is one of the most important texts in Tibetan Buddhism and is studied in monastic colleges and by the four major schools: Nyingma, Kagyu, Sakya, and Gelug[3]. It emphasizes the importance of the Three Jewels, that is, the Buddha, Dharma (the Teachings), and Sangha (spiritual community) and discusses the notion of karma and various other topics that are both philosophically important and related to actual practices within Buddhism. This text provides a good balance between theory and practical advice. There are many different commentaries written on Letter to a Friend in both Indian and Tibetan languages. This commentary relates to an Indian version written by Aryadeva, a student of Nagarjuna. It is a text used by commentators from the four major Tibetan schools.

Nagarjuna was one of the founders of Mahayana Buddhism[4]. Mahayana Buddhism is a later form of Buddhism that spread to many countries including China, Tibet, and Japan and became the established form of Buddhism in those countries. Nagarjuna is treated with great reverence by Tibetans and most people come to know about him through his philosophical writings. This is not a philosophical text as such, but rather a text that covers the whole gamut of Buddhist theory and practice. According to modern Western historians, proof of a King Gautamiputra as a historical figure can be found in the ancient archives of India and his reign corresponds to the time the Letter to a Friend was composed. Letter to a Friend is written in verse form followed by a commentary.

Encouragement to Listen to the Teachings

By accumulating virtuous deeds you have become wholesome and noble.
Thus creating the conditions to hear these concise Arya[5] *verses*
Which I have composed so you may apprehend their meaning
Arising from contemplating the Sugata's words.

The word *Sugata* means the "Buddha" and refers to the Buddha's words. Aryadeva states that this particular verse brings out the importance of several points. Firstly, Nagarjuna informs the king he has some kind of connection to the Buddha. It is not by accident that the encounter between Nagarjuna and the king took place. There was some kind of unspoken bond between the two that came about because of their past connections, particularly in terms of the king's own past deeds. After meeting with Nagarjuna, the king had transformed himself into what is described as a "proper vessel" to contain the teachings of the Buddha. When Nagarjuna says to the king that he is a person of great virtue, he is implying their meeting was no accident and the king was put in a fortunate circumstance because of what had passed earlier, especially in terms of the king's wholesome and noble deeds. Therefore, the king could become a proper vessel to contain the teachings of the Buddha.

Secondly, Nagarjuna intends to be very succinct. At the end of the verse, Nagarjuna says he is going to be very brief with regard to what he has to say as the king has many tasks to attend to and being very busy, may not have the leisure to do many hours of study. The king needs something very succinct and condensed but at the same time, something that has all the necessary instructions of a manual. Therefore, Nagarjuna states that what follows is to the point and there will be no elaborate descriptions of subtle philosophical points. Finally, Nagarjuna refers to himself in the following verse:

> I am the one responsible for composing this text and I will explain it in a very succinct fashion to you. You are quite fortunate to receive these teachings because they are the teachings of the Buddha. The teachings of the Buddha are worthwhile contemplating. The teachings of the Buddha are endowed with the power to bestow liberation on you, the king, and everybody else who may happen to read this text because this text contains the teachings of the Sugata, the Buddha himself.

Focus on the Meaning of the Teachings

If an image of the Sugata is made roughly out of wood,
The low quality image should not affect one's awe of the Buddha's wisdom.
Similarly, though these verses I have composed lack grace do not negate them
As they contain essential aspects of the Buddha's teachings.

According to Aryadeva, Nagarjuna is trying to say he is not particularly concerned about the poetic elegance or lack thereof of his composition, but rather more concerned with the content of what he is writing. If anyone should say he has not written this very well, Nagarjuna's response is that it is not meant to prove his skill in poetic composition, but rather to convey the teachings of the Buddha in an effective manner. In this particular verse, Nagarjuna states that a sacred statue like that of the Buddha is revered by everyone and that thoughtful people revere such a figurine and usually think of it as being very precious. It is not because of the material used to fashion the statue or how much it is worth in terms of the monetary value, but what it represents. Even if it were not very well made, people would not even engage in a discussion about the aesthetic beauty of the statue or the ugliness of it, saying, "This Buddha statue is really despicable, it's so revolting." People would still show respect for such an artifact.

In a similar manner, Nagarjuna states that people should not judge this particular text based upon how it is written but on its content. One should be thinking about what is being said and whether it is worthwhile and carries any real significance rather than spending time looking at the arrangement of the text. Nagarjuna's point is that when we are reading this text, we should be paying attention to the meaning of those words. What the words mean is more important than the words themselves or how the words are organized and arranged. Even if one does not think much of the text in terms of its literary quality, nevertheless it is still worthwhile paying attention to because of what the text is about, as well as the intention behind the text and the effect intended by the author.

The Importance of Learning

No matter how often you have heard the Conqueror Sugata's words
Even if you have understood them well continue to listen with intent
Just like seeing a beautiful mansion made of white marble
Its luminosity is enhanced when seen under the light of a midnight moon.

One of the epithets bestowed on the Buddha is "Conqueror" so "the words of the Conqueror" means somebody who has mastered what are known as the *three gates of one's being*, namely body, speech, and mind. Consequently, one has been able to abandon all of the conflicting emotions and their causes and the underlying latent causes and conditions in terms of psychic imprints. The words of a Conqueror of this kind are full of meaning and significance and are also very easy and pleasant to listen to. Nagarjuna's point is that the words of a teacher such as the Buddha may not be completely alien to the king who may already be quite informed without having to listen to Nagarjuna speak on similar topics. Another point he makes is that it may very well be the case that the king may be more familiar with such topics than a layperson insofar as his spiritual training and education are concerned, but knowledge such as this is something that one can continue to accumulate.

One cannot put a stop to spiritual education and training and say, "Now my training is sufficient. It is complete and I know enough now so I don't need to learn anymore." One is unable to do this because whatever illumination one may have been able to gain up to this point is a tremendous achievement in itself but going further will shed even more light on the things the king may still be uncertain about. According to Aryadeva, Nagarjuna makes this point with the following analogy. He asks the king to imagine a mansion made of white marble, a mansion which is already very vibrant and luminous so that on a clear night this could be seen in the distance—and if the moon comes out and shines on the marble palace, then it will look even more grand. It will shimmer and radiate even more light, making what was a very beautiful palace look even more beautiful.

Similarly, adding more knowledge to the existing body of knowledge brings even more illumination and understanding, even if one has knowledge of spiritual matters to begin with. This is the attitude that the king and readers of this text should have and not think, "I have heard about similar sorts of things. I myself have thought about these sorts of things before." One should not have that attitude but instead should listen to the text with a sense of openness.

This completes the preliminary remarks regarding the text.

The Main Body of the Text

Pursuing the Virtuous Life

The main body of the text itself begins with the next verse. This verse gives counsel to both ordained and laypeople who are interested in the Dharma by highlighting the importance of showing respect to the "Triple Gem" in Buddhism, namely, the Buddha, Dharma, and Sangha.

The Six Reminders

Bring to mind the six recollections taught by the Conqueror:
The triple gem—the Buddha, his teachings, and community;
Generosity, ethics, and the enlightenment mind.
Contemplate the qualities of the six for inspiration on the path.

This particular section is explained in three stages:

a. Nagarjuna counsels the king and would-be readers of this text to pursue a virtuous life.
b. Nagarjuna warns readers of the fallibility of the samsaric condition.
c. Nagarjuna gives counsel on the importance of striving towards nirvana or nirvanic liberation.

According to Aryadeva, this particular verse refers to both the teaching methods for ordained people and for laypeople like the king. Regardless of whether they are ordained or not, Nagarjuna states that they must practice what are called the "*six recollections*" (*dran pa drug*) in Tibetan. The first three, the Buddha or the enlightened teacher, the Dharma or the teachings of the Enlightened One, and the Sangha or the members of the community who follow those teachings, are of utmost importance. As mentioned earlier, the Buddha is given many different epithets, one of which is the word, "*sang gye*" (*sangs rgyas*) in Tibetan, meaning Enlightened One. The other is *gyal wa* (*rgyal ba*), which means Victorious One. Aryadeva says that the Buddha is called "*gyalwa*" meaning "victorious" which means the Buddha has overcome and conquered all the inhibiting factors within himself and all the self-defeating attitudes and tendencies. Therefore, the Buddha's capacity to enact and apply himself is greatly increased.

The word sang gye: "*sang*" means the Buddha has managed to rid himself of all the confusion, conflicting emotions, and debilitating tendencies and "*gye*" means all the positive qualities one would wish to develop have become developed; it has the connotation of flowering. The Buddha has managed to achieve both—to be rid of all of those unhelpful and debilitating tendencies and to reach full maturity by acquiring all the good qualities one requires to be a fully rounded person. The Buddha has spoken about the importance of the *six reminders* and throughout one's life one should think about these and other qualities of a Buddha.

We need inspiration and encouragement in order to stay on course once we have chosen and embarked on the spiritual path we want to follow. Such inspiration and encouragement we can receive from the buddhas. By thinking about the buddhas, the Enlightened Ones, and their attainments, we become inspired, we wish to go ahead and continue to advance on our path. This is exactly what the buddhas of the past have had to do. When we think about the qualities of the Buddha we can think about the individual qualities that the Buddha or the Enlightened Ones possess.

Recollecting the Qualities of the Buddha

1. The first is the quality of subjugation. The Buddha is the greatest subjugator of all without the use of violence. Buddha has been able to overcome all that is troublesome or demeaning and all that is vile and destructive has been pacified. This is why Buddha is also referred to as "*chom den de*" (*bcom ldan das*) in Tibetan, which means one who has subdued all the troubling forces.

2. The second quality is the Buddha's understanding. One should think not only about Buddha's capacity in terms of showing great fortitude and even-mindedness. A buddha has skill in terms of managing emotions and great capacity in terms of their cognitive ability. Buddha manifests superior cognitive abilities, something that non-buddhas do not have.

3. A quality that the Buddha also has is the capacity to communicate in a way that always leads to rapprochement and understanding and does not lead to misunderstanding, confusion, and deception.

4. Another quality that the Buddha possesses is the capacity to behave in an impeccable fashion, meaning that Buddha always knows how to behave appropriately given different circumstances.

5. One of the other qualities the Buddha possesses is the development of a very high level of attainment so that there is no possibility of regression. Unlike our normal attempts to improve ourselves or to do certain things, where we manage up to a point, but if we rest content with that we fall back to where we were before, where this possibility does not exist for a Buddha. A Buddha's position is secured.

Once attained, there is no possibility of regression and this is another unique attainment of Buddha.

6. Finally, Buddha has the capacity to work with other beings in most ingenious ways and in the most skillful manner possible.

Aryadeva states that the Buddha's capacity to work with beings in the most skillful and ingenious ways is explained in Buddhist literature using the analogy of a chariot-driver. A skilled chariot-driver of course has to work with different kinds of horses and has to know horses very well. Somebody who does not know or understand horses would not be a good chariot-driver and would fail as a driver. Different horses have different temperaments and behave differently, so in order to get through to the horse, the chariot-driver has to be skillful. There are certain steps that the chariot-driver has to take in order to get the horse to the desired level. In a similar fashion, Buddha does the same thing with different sentient beings.

Sentient beings are also very varied with very different predilections, personalities, temperaments, needs, and aspirations. A chariot-driver will first try to make the horse become comfortable with the harness and then has to see if the horse will be comfortable drawing the chariot and staying on course. This also involves a lot of skill. Just using the whip is not the answer and many different methods have to be applied. Sometimes the horse may have such a temperament that some kind of exchange is necessary between the charioteer and the horse. Sometimes one may have a horse that is very stubborn and recalcitrant and in such a case the charioteer may give the horse a break and leave it alone for a while. The charioteer uses many different methods like this. The Buddha also does a similar kind of thing because he wants to make sure people are on the path to enlightenment. The Buddha wants to put everybody on the path to enlightenment but as people are very different, they will follow that path in different ways. The Buddha has to accommodate this and cover the discrepancies in terms of people's needs, aspirations, personalities, and temperaments. For example, this may also mean that if somebody is completely against being given advice or against the notion any kind of spirituality, then the Buddha may not insist on compliance in a very blatant fashion but may treat that person with indifference.

Recollecting the Qualities of the Buddha's Teachings

According to Aryadeva, the main point to consider is that the Buddha has a unique ability to communicate and work with a wide variety of beings. This is something ordinary people such as ourselves lack but have the potential to develop. One should try to become inspired to follow that kind of example and seek refuge in that kind of being by thinking about and reminding oneself of the qualities the Buddha possesses. We should then think about the Dharma, which are the teachings the Buddha taught. If buddhas possess the kinds of qualities that have been broadly listed, then it stands to reason that whatever such a being teaches is going to be something worth paying attention to and will bring great benefit to oneself. If buddhas and bodhisattvas have these qualities, then their teachings are going to be of equal importance. This is exactly what we should be thinking. Buddha's teachings are not just teachings that somebody with a little bit of wisdom gave; they are the teachings of an enlightened one. The teachings are the words spoken by enlightened beings and are based on true insight. The Buddha saw things clearly and therefore whatever he spoke is based on that clarity. The Buddha's teachings are free of any kind of disease and do not lead to further disturbances of the mind or personality, meaning that the teachings always lead to satisfactory conclusions or results.

As the Buddha's teachings operate on many different levels and are not completely dependent upon spoken and written words, they are also preserved in a way that is not easily damaged through fluctuations in the material world. A part of the teachings is recorded in the deep recesses of the human mind itself and especially in the minds of enlightened beings. The Buddha's teachings therefore bestow meaning on those who are confused and undergoing great personal upheaval and misery. Just like the Buddha, the Buddha's teachings are wide and varied so there is tremendous variety to be found in the teachings; there is something for everyone. This is why sometimes in the teachings it is said that Buddha's teachings are good at the beginning, good in the middle, and good at the end. Real teachings are actualized through the practice of meditation. The teaching one learns through the inculcation of the written word becomes merged with one's own continuum, the continuum of one's being.

This means the Buddha's teachings can be basically grouped into two categories:

a. The first kind corresponds to the first two of the four noble truths: The Truth of Suffering and the Truth of the Cause of Suffering.

b. The last two correspond to the teachings that are cognitively assimilated within oneself, so that the Truth of Cessation and the Truth of the Way Out of Suffering are incorporated into that. In this way, Buddha's teachings are not simply assimilated through cogitation alone but through a proper assimilation of those teachings so that they lead directly to self-realization.

Further qualities of the teachings are also mentioned in the text. One of the most important things about the teachings is that they do clarify. There are many things we can learn about and some of these can cause more confusion than clarity. By properly studying the Buddha's teachings they will clarify and bring illumination in the mind. It is important to note there is both subjective clarification and objective clarification.

1. Subjective clarification arises from gaining insight. Our mind becomes more perspicacious and lucid through the assimilation of the teachings.
2. Objective illumination comes from gaining more understanding of what reality is.
3. The third form of clarification comes from the removal of the contradictory and conflicting experiences that we may have.

There is clarification in the mind because it becomes less and less deluded. As we gain more understanding of the teachings through practice, there is a lightening up of our mind and the delusions begin to thin out. When the delusions and defilements begin to lessen, we are able to renounce them for good. It is not that we reduce them and they come back to haunt us again. This is the meaning of the third noble truth; the Truth of Cessation. The Truth of Cessation means that all of the disturbing things in the mind that cloud our judgment and disrupt our ability to see things properly are eradicated. Instead, we become endowed with what is called discriminating wisdom or discriminating awareness. We begin to develop the ability to discern things very clearly and become less subject to our whimsical moods that allow us to be swayed by our impulses and delusional thoughts. Armed with such a wisdom mind we are able to resolve any contradictory notions that we may be holding. We are able to let go of all the conflicting things that we may be hanging onto. All conflict will come to rest if one gains some insight into the true nature of things. These are some of the qualities that the Dharma or teachings possess.

We should recall and try to think about this during the course of our lives. We can think about how fantastic and wonderful an enlightened being is and what an exceptional being a Buddha is. We can also think about the profundity, the effectiveness, and the remedial quality of the teachings. The teachings possess the dual quality of bringing illumination as well as transformation. Sometimes we may have insight, but it is not translated into transformation and sometimes there may be some form of transformation, but no insight. The Dharma teachings are able to accomplish both. One becomes endowed with insight and the insight leads to transformation.

Recollecting the Qualities of the Sangha

One should also think about the importance of the Sangha or the community of practitioners who follow the dharmic path. There are many different kinds of Sangha members but in this context, we can speak about the Sangha members of the ordained variety who have taken on monk or nun vows. One should think of the qualities of real Sangha members; what qualities a genuine Sangha member would have. A Sangha member is training in the three aspects of their being which are their body, speech, and mind. A real Sangha member does not simply try to preserve and observe the vows, but is trying to cultivate themselves mentally and spiritually as well.

In the Buddhist literature about monastic vows or the *Vinaya*, a great deal of time is spent speaking about the qualities the different Sangha members must possess. They must be able to get along with the lay community and so a lot of time is spent on the importance of Sangha members maintaining respectability. The members of the lay community who see a Sangha member should immediately be inspired by seeing that monk or nun as somebody to look up to because of that particular person's demeanor and conduct. The lay community would then want to support Sangha members.

Therefore, Sangha members must possess the quality of respectability that is earned through great diligence through the observation of monastic vows and in terms of self-cultivation.

The way this is explained in the Buddhist cultural context and literature is that it is the duty of the lay members to support Sangha members and the duty of the Sangha is to make themselves respectable and not allow themselves to become corrupted. A Sangha member should try to keep the vows intact and not become too caught up with worldly affairs. One should remain autonomous, be learned, do a sufficient amount of meditative practice, and try to work continuously on whatever faults or defects one might have in one's character. We should think about the Sangha in that fashion. The Sangha should be thought of as being populated by people with high ideals who are living a life devoted to self-improvement and community service. The Sangha members' duty is to help the lay community in terms of fulfilling their needs. In any case, one should think about the Triple Gem in this way.

In Buddhism, the Triple Gem is held as the ultimate symbol of spiritual authority and spiritual power. The legitimacy or authenticity of the practice has to be drawn from these three different sources in whatever one does as a Buddhist. There would be no Dharma and no Sangha without the Buddha. If we respect the Buddha then we have to respect the Dharma and if we respect the Dharma we have to respect the Sangha. It is through understanding the Dharma that the buddhas become enlightened and the Dharma is kept alive by the body of practitioners or Sangha. In this way the teachings are kept alive and the possibility for attaining enlightenment does not become extinct. As Buddhist practitioners, it is of the utmost importance to keep reminding ourselves of these. According to Aryadeva, as Nagarjuna has made a big point of this to the king, these three points are important things to be considered.

The *six reminders* are the Buddha, Dharma, and Sangha and refer to Buddha Shakyamuni, his teachings, and the Sangha are those who follow Shakyamuni's teachings. As the unique qualities of the Triple Gem have already been discussed, the three remaining reminders are the practice of generosity, moral precepts, and the reminder that relates to the qualities of gods. These will be explained in more detail in the course of the text.

At a basic level, these three suggest that somebody who is following the Dharma who wants to lead a life guided by the Triple Gem needs to learn to practice generosity on all different levels, both in terms of practice and also in terms of one's psychological attitudes. One should also learn to practice moral precepts in addition to this. This means the individual should pay attention to things that one should refrain from doing. One should learn to refrain from those things that are harmful, while also trying to do things that are beneficial in relation to what is positive. Finally, one should try to cultivate one's mind, particularly in terms of refining one's mental states. This is achieved through the practice of samadhi or meditative concentration which is what is meant by the "reminder of the gods" referring to the gods of the form and formless realms as discussed in the Buddhist teachings.

If one engages in meditative concentration, one can attain what are called "divine mental states" or the mind of a form god or formless god: this is a key point. When one is practicing meditation one can reach these very high levels of meditative states, which are very refined states of mind. The first three reminders are used as a guide and the three remaining reminders have to do with practice. According to Nagarjuna, the individual practitioner (who in this case is the king) should think of these *six reminders* all the time.

The actual practices are discussed in more detail in the following verses whereby the next verse describes those things we should refrain from.

Counsel to Remain Steadfast in One's Virtuous Conduct

Aspire to act according to the ten virtuous deeds
Cultivated through body, speech, and mind.
Practicing moderation of intoxicants and
Rejoice in the wholesomeness of a non-harming livelihood.

Using the *six reminders*, the serious Buddhist individual who wants to embark on the dharmic path first of all has to learn how to lead a wholesome life, a good life. Leading a good life has to do with the coincidence of the ideal that one wants to achieve and the satisfaction of one's desires. Following a livelihood based on refraining from the ten non-virtuous deeds and the cultivation of the ten virtuous deeds leads to the experience of the coincidence of aspiration and satisfaction of one's desires. In other words, we have certain ideals and desires that we want to satisfy but due to our confusion and overwhelming conflicting emotions and a predominance of ignorance, we are unable to meet them.

An individual who wants to lead a wholesome life that will lead to the attainment of one's ideals should lead a life that involves the avoidance of the ten non-virtuous deeds and cultivate the ten virtuous deeds. If our ideals are based on genuineness, there would be a relationship between the virtues that we cultivate and the ideals that we want to attain. In order to do that, we have to think about ourselves in relation to our body, speech, and mind. How we live is based on the use of these three things: how we make use of the body, how we make use of speech, and how we make use of our mind. So that before one can actually think about cultivating the virtues we need to cultivate, we have to think about avoiding the things that are harmful to us and to others.

Reflecting on Karma

The ideal we want to attain is liberation from suffering. We want to attain a state that is not only free of suffering but is also endowed with all kinds of possibilities of fulfillment. First one has to learn to avoid things that would prevent one from achieving attaining this goal in order to achieve the full consummation of one's potentialities. Physically one has to learn to avoid doing things like killing, unnecessarily taking the life of insects and small creatures, stealing and taking things from others that do not belong to oneself, and improper engagement in sexual conduct. These things are a constant source of disruption in our lives. If we continue to indulge in these things we cannot have a fulfilling life or aim towards attaining our goal. We will not attain our true ideal, nor will we be able to satisfy our desires. As will be explained in due course, even though we may think that we are able to satisfy our desires through indulging in these activities, we only exacerbate our experience of actual and potential frustration and manage to cause further disruption in our lives. It also has the effect of gradually having a negative impact on our character. As virtue is built on our character, if we do not have strong character, we leave ourselves open for all the vices and viciousness in our nature to take full possession. Trying not to kill, steal, or engage in sexual misconduct and things of that kind are what one needs to practice.

What one has to understand is that there is a close connection between one's mental state and one's behavior change. It is something one needs to pay attention to. How one behaves, the sort of behavior we indulge in will either encourage or discourage certain emotional upheavals from occurring and have the effect of exacerbating or reducing the negative impact of these emotional upheavals. If we indulge in practices like taking life or telling lies and things of that kind, this directly relates to our mental state and will stir up all kinds of negative states of mind and negative emotions. These kinds of actions lead to corruption in one's character and to the creation of negative karma. The way in which practices like this that are concerned with the physical, verbal, or mental aspects of our actions and how they relate to karma, is actually quite complex.

Although there is a connection between our mental states and our physical and verbal forms of action, how they come together determines whether we are going to create negative karma or not. If there are conflicting emotions in our mind, such as hatred for example, a negative mental state has already arisen. If one is propelled to act in some way and this is realized in the performance of an action and a negative action is created, nevertheless, it does not qualify as the full completion of a negative form of action. For a negative form of action to occur, the intention needs to be present as well. Therefore, there has to be some kind of preparation or intention to perform this action in addition to the presence of the negative form of emotion. Two elements are missing: the motivation and the preparation, "*jar wa*" (*sbyar ba*) in Tibetan.

In other words, the more deliberate an action, the graver the consequence of the karma that action carries. Even if there is some form of negative emotion present, if the motivation and preparation for the completion of the act are not present, then this does not result in a full-blown karmic effect. One has to think about karmic cause and effect with more intelligence and is something one has to become informed of. Sometimes the negative emotion may be present, the intention to do harm is present, and one may even have made preparation. If a strong intention to do harm is present but the act is not carried out, then it is not a full-blown karmic act. It does not eventuate or result in full fructification of the karmic effect. In other words, we create our real negative karma through body, speech, and mind when a negative state of mind is present, when the motivation and preparedness or strong intention to do harm is present, and when the action is performed. When all of these things come together we have created real negative karma through our body, speech, and mind.

Through our body we create negative karma by killing, stealing, and things of that kind. Through speech we create negative karma by lying, causing friction between people, gossiping, and things of that kind. Through mind we create negative karma by covetousness, wanting to do harm to others, and holding wrong views about things. The main point seems to be that the object has to be present and there has to be a negative state of mind with negative motivation, intention, and the performance of the action. We succeed in creating negative karma when all of these factors come together. It is not sufficient that we want to kill someone and that we have the intention and the negative state of mind; the object has to be there. If there is no sentient being immediately present whose life may be threatened or in danger, that karmic deed is not concluded.

In any case, Nagarjuna has said we need to understand that all these things coming together have a corroding effect on our character and it would be very difficult for us to develop virtue. These virtues are connected to securing the ideals that we want to attain. Therefore, trying to avoid indulging in negative forms of action is of paramount importance. In this particular context, action includes acts performed through our body, speech or verbal action, and mind. We have to understand this in relation to all the negative actions to do with physical, verbal, and mental actions. For example, if we are talking about stealing, there has to be an object that we covet and want and so the object has to be present. This has to be followed by the motivation to possess that object and then one has to be moved to steal it; one actually has to steal the object. When this series of acts is performed and the series is completed we have committed the negative karma of stealing.

As mentioned previously, to refrain from doing these things is one thing but if we try to save life instead of killing or if two people are fighting and we make the effort to mend that friendship, then we are performing virtuous actions. We are doing the opposite of what we were doing when we were performing negative forms of action. Instead of stealing, the practice of generosity is encouraged, in addition to trying to refrain from certain things. We should also delight in a wholesome livelihood. To delight in a wholesome livelihood means trying to live one's life based on doing the opposite to what we may normally be compelled to do. These two things are seen as being quite separate. First one has to learn not to do certain things even if we want to and then afterwards try to do the opposite. According to Nagarjuna, indulging in intoxicants like alcohol is also discouraged, not because alcohol or intoxicants in themselves are evil but because of the effect alcohol or other forms of intoxicants may have on one's mind. One may lose one's mind in a state of intoxication and be propelled to indulge in forms of action that one would not indulge in normally if one were sober. Therefore, one should refrain from this also.

Of the ten non-virtues or forms of negative action that one has to refrain from, three are related to body, four are related to speech, and three are related to the mind. The three of body are killing, inappropriate sexual conduct, and stealing. The four non-virtues of speech are spreading lies, indulging in gossip, speaking aggressive words, and causing friction between people by doing things such as telling one thing to one person and saying something else to another person behind their backs. Mentally, the three non-virtues are covetousness, coveting others money or whatever others may have, wanting to do harm and holding onto wrong views. Wrong views will be explained further in due course. Some examples of wrong views are views that hold that trying to refrain from these kinds of actions will not lead to having fulfilling experiences and that there is no connection between our actions and what we become or what we experience later in life. Thinking in this way is considered to be a wrong view in Buddhism.

As mentioned, intoxicants lead to "*bag me*" (*bag med*) in Tibetan, which means carelessness. As the use of intoxicants leads to carelessness and recklessness, this is also something to be avoided. In addition, we should try as much as possible to do the opposite of all that. Also as previously mentioned, physically we should try to save lives, and verbally we try to mend friendships instead of gossiping and things of this kind.. We also try to speak about things that are important and meaningful. Instead of wanting to do harm to others, we try to think well of others. Nagarjuna says that a wholesome livelihood follows from trying to learn to do these kinds of things. Nagarjuna further expands on this point so that one can practice these things properly.

Recollection of Generosity

> *Knowing that wealth is unstable and devoid of essence*
> *Rightly bestow gifts upon monks, Brahmans*
> *The poor, and friends; so for the next life*
> *There is no more excellent a kinsman than giving.*

The previous verse concerns what not to do if we are really serious about wanting to lead a fulfilling life and attain the goals that we have set for ourselves as practitioners, while also explaining what should be done instead. According to Nagarjuna, the most important thing one should do is learn to practice generosity. Human beings have an overwhelming experience of feeling poverty-stricken, with an insatiable desire for the things that they want to have. Nagarjuna states this is completely unhelpful and that to be in that state is very, very disturbing for the individual. For one thing, material things in terms of property and money do not have any substantiality. When it is said that they are insubstantial, this means that they do not last and whatever is there can be lost. According to Nagarjuna, material things cannot be a source of security. Our fortunes fluctuate and therefore cannot be relied upon because they are non-substantial. They do not provide security because they themselves fluctuate and are impermanent by nature.

Nagarjuna states that material things should be used as a means to improve oneself through learning to be generous with them. One should try to help those who need help. If one can afford it, one should try to help somebody who has devoted their life to spirituality and relies upon others for sustenance. People who have devoted their lives to practice such as monks and Brahmins are not in the business of making money for themselves and should be helped. According to Nagarjuna, learning to be generous is the very foundation of all of one's moral practices. Generosity will not only serve us well while we are alive but at the time of death and in the future. We will be aided by the practice of generosity. If we practice generosity it will become easier to cultivate the other virtues. If a person is very greedy and has a poverty-stricken attitude, all the other virtuous qualities are very difficult to develop. If one has a sense of magnanimity and is giving and forthcoming both materially and in terms of how one conducts oneself and interacts with others and is not overprotective, territorial, or possessive, but very outgoing, then all of these things will be helped along by being generous. One will then become more approachable and friendly towards others and all the other virtuous qualities will quickly follow.

Recollection of Moral Precepts

If one has vowed to refrain from particular types of behavior
Maintain that vow well and without subversion.
Holding a moral precept is the foundation of all virtue,
Just as the earth is the ground upon which both animate and inanimate stand.

Based on the practice of generosity one should try to practice moral precepts[6]. "Moral precepts" here does not just mean morality. It is one thing to say to oneself, "I will not kill," or "I will not eat meat," or "I will not smoke cigarettes and drink alcohol," or whatever. It is another thing to actually take a precept and say, "For a period of time I will not take life deliberately and knowingly," and try to stick to that. This is what is referred to by "moral precepts." Nagarjuna explains this in more detail later in his Letter in terms of how a layperson can take precepts or how monks or nuns in terms of their vows can take precepts. It is still called a moral precept whether one takes the vows of a monk or a lay precept that lasts only for a day. The taking of precepts can also be strengthened through the practice of generosity.

The Practice of Taking Moral Precepts

The first thing one needs to do is make sure one does not take too many precepts to begin with, saying, "I will not do this and I will not do that," while knowing one will not be able to keep them. One should be judicious and selective in the reasons one chooses to take precepts. For example, if something has become a big problem and one thinks that one should refrain from doing it and wishes to stop doing it, then one should stick to that, making sure that one does not violate the precepts one has taken. Not violating the precepts is one of the main points. The second point concerning precepts is their use as a "sort of lid" to not allow the undesirable aspects of oneself from flourishing. In other words, if there is a behavior that one has a problem with and one has taken a precept that one is not going to do it, this puts a lid on that. However if one continues to indulge in the behavior, it will only get worse. It may even manifest in other ways. For example, if one has a preponderance to kill, then first one may kill all kinds of insects and so forth for no reason, and one may graduate to killing animals, and from that to killing human beings, and so it proliferates. If one takes a precept, this puts a lid on that opening and whatever tendency one may have will not get worse.

When one has taken a precept, one should also try to keep pure motivation and not allow the precept to get mixed up with negative states of mind or negative emotions.

When one takes a precept one should take it in a genuine manner. We should not just do it for the sake of somebody else. If somebody finds a certain behavior in us unpalatable, then we might take precepts and stop doing whatever it might be, although Nagarjuna says this is not a good reason to refrain from certain behaviors. We should not take precepts for the sake of the approval of others or even because of some material gain. One should refrain from certain behaviors for oneself. One should think this genuinely has a long-lasting benefit for one's situation. This will open the way to liberation and increase one's sense of autonomy and one will feel less enslaved to one's impulses and habit patterns.

The other associated benefit we could have from taking precepts is they will have a sort of calming effect on oneself if we are attentive to them. Therefore, the next time we are meditating we will be less agitated and restless and this will also help one meditate better. In other words, whatever can be done to stop disturbing behavior from continuing will then automatically have a positive effect on oneself. This will also help one to have a calmer demeanor and one can meditate more easily.

These points refer to the reason why it is said that the taking of moral precepts is a very good way to learn to improve one's character. Taking precepts should be seen as the very foundation of the building of one's character. As Nagarjuna states, this is compared to the earth itself. The earth supports all living creatures and everything else, even inanimate things like mountains and rivers. Apart from the practice of generosity, this is the second thing that one should think about. One should practice normally in this way, but one may want to practice more than this. This is the standard Buddhist approach to leading a wholesome life. Nagarjuna states that if one wants to follow the Mahayana path, one may wish to practice other things besides what has been said so far in terms of refraining from non-virtuous deeds, the cultivation of virtuous deeds, and the practice of generosity and moral precepts. One should practice the *six paramitas* if one wants to follow the bodhisattva path of Mahayana. This point is explained in the next verse.

Practicing the Six Perfections of Mahayana

Increase the practices of generosity, moral precepts,
Patience, vigor, meditative concentration, and wisdom.
Accumulation of such merit transforms the samsaric mind
to seeking benefit for all, thus the traveller reaches the enlightened shore.

A Mahayana practitioner tries to practice the six paramitas[7] These are called the six paramitas because the practice of generosity and moral precepts in this context is different from what has been discussed so far. A Mahayana practitioner wants to practice generosity and moral precepts with *bodhicitta* in mind. Bodhicitta means "enlightened heart" and enlightened heart is generated by thinking of the welfare of all sentient beings. Whatever spiritual practice one engages in, one does not do it simply for one's own sake. One is doing it for the sake of others as well. The idea is, "If I practice generosity not only would I get benefit, but others would also benefit from it. If I advance on the path and become more liberated, then I will have the opportunity or capacity to help others. I will acquire the ability, so I will be able to help them more."

By thinking in this way, one engages in the six paramita practice; the practice of generosity, moral precepts, patience, vigor, meditative concentration, and wisdom. Nagarjuna says that when the bodhisattva, "*jang jub kye sem*" (*byang chub kyi sems*) in Tibetan, practices generosity, one is not thinking about oneself, the other individual, the object of one's generosity, or the act of generosity. One is simply doing a beneficial thing because it is the thing to do. It is beneficial. One practices moral precepts in the same way. A bodhisattva is someone who is not afraid or timid in terms of extending themselves. Through the practice of mind-training and things of that kind, the bodhisattva tries to transform difficulties and utilize adverse circumstances and situations on the path as part of one's practice. One does not get discouraged and with the use of vigor or "*virya*" (Skt.) one is able to maintain one's enthusiasm.

For the virtues to flourish, one has to have enthusiasm and enthusiasm has to come from wanting to do all of these things. One is not thinking of these as being a burden or a duty that one is performing. The bodhisattva is happy to be practicing generosity and the virtue of patience. The virtues are practiced because the bodhisattva wants to and not because the bodhisattva *has* to perform them. The energy level is always up. The bodhisattva also practices meditative concentration and cultivates insight or wisdom through the practice of meditation and contemplation, as will be explained further on in the text. From the Mahayana point of view, the way to conduct oneself is to follow the six paramitas, which is slightly different from what has been said in the previous two verses. The six paramitas can be followed by everyone: whether one is a layperson or an ordained person does not matter.

In Mahayana Buddhism, the six paramitas are practiced because character is an important factor in terms of how much enjoyment and satisfaction one is getting from one's life and how one is living. For this to happen, two things are mentioned: the accumulation of merit and the accumulation of wisdom. The first one, the accumulation of merit, comes from the practice of generosity, moral precepts, patience, and vigor. This means when we are impoverished in terms of our merit, we attract negativity. All kinds of bad things happen to us. When merit is created there is a real transformation within ourselves and we become enriched. Due to a lack of merit, we become impoverished and due to merit, we become enriched. Therefore, merit is an important factor. We accomplish the second one, the accumulation of wisdom, through the practices of meditation and contemplation. Meditation helps us with meditative concentration and contemplation helps us to develop insight and wisdom.

As it has been explained in the Mahayana literature, when we have merit, everything about us exudes a sense of confidence and positivity, but we experience all kinds of disturbances from both within and without when our life is thrown into a state of lack of merit. In our mind, we feel disturbances and in terms of our environment, we experience disturbances of one kind or another. With regard to the attainment of Buddhahood, another point the Mahayana practitioner tries to remember is that if we accumulate merit, this directly leads to the attainment of Buddha's physical body and the accumulation of wisdom is transformed into the mind of the Buddha. The two aspects of Buddha's being, which are the physical and mental aspects, result from these two different kinds of accumulations. These two accumulations also lead to a very balanced life because four of the six paramitas help us to focus our mind on this world and the two remaining paramitas help us to focus our mind on the transcendental realm. Due to wisdom we are able to have direct insight into the reality of things and because of compassion, which is materialized through the practice of generosity, moral precepts, patience, and vigor, we are able to effectively lead a fulfilling life.

This concludes the general description of what one needs to do as a Buddhist practitioner.

Remaining Steadfast in Virtue

General Advice for Laypeople Practicing Dharma

At the beginning level when one pursues the Buddhist path, what should one focus on? After thinking about the importance of the Triple Gem, Buddha, Dharma, and Sangha, what is the next step? The next step is to think about leading a life based on the cultivation of virtue and the overcoming of non-virtue in the context of both the Mahayana and non-Mahayana. Before one can train in the Buddhist practice of meditation and contemplation on the realization of one's true nature or ultimate reality, first one has to found one's practice on sound moral and ethical values. As previously explained, in Buddhism, there are three different practices: the practice of ethics and morality, the practice of meditative concentration, and the practice of the cultivation of wisdom. Meditation will not take root if one is leading a life that is totally chaotic. Learning to lead a life that is beneficial both for oneself and for others helps one to meditate. If one cannot meditate, it is not possible to gain insight into one's true nature or into the nature of ultimate reality because one's mind would still be in a state of turmoil.

A precondition for the development of wisdom is to have a sound and workable mind. In this way, Nagarjuna proposes that someone coming to Buddhist practice firstly has to consider the sorts of things one should try to avoid and those one should cultivate. If there are certain things one has a big problem with in terms of one's behavior or habits, one may even want to take a precept or a vow. One may take a vow of celibacy or a precept of not taking life or of not drinking alcohol, even if just for a day or a week or a month. Doing these things will help in trying to integrate the virtuous practices so that they collectively have an impact on one's mind. There is very little point in engaging in wholesome activity only to allow some kind of negative emotion to spill over and corrupt the practice. One has to try to keep the balance and if one does meditation and cultivates insight this will help.

Before one does this, Nagarjuna has some further advice on how laypeople should go about their daily business while trying to practice the Dharma, such as when one is trying to perform normal duties as a householder. What he has been saying is fairly straightforward and therefore very clear. This has to do with trying to understand Buddhist practices in relation to the Buddhist practice of meditation. Often we may do some meditation every day or at least a few times a week and we may be hoping that this will be sufficient for us to experience all the things the teachings say we should be experiencing. If that doesn't happen we may think the Buddhist practices, or the Buddhist teachings do not work. As Nagarjuna makes very clear, we have to have a Buddhist approach to life. We have to try to do the whole thing and only then can we expect the teachings to work. It's not like we do half-an-hour of meditation whenever we can and then think, "This has to help me overcome all my negative habits or all the undesirable things I experience. They should just disappear and if they don't disappear then the Buddhist practices obviously do not work," or something. It has to be an integrated approach.

Buddhist theory (if it can be called this) regarding moral or ethical values is not moralistic. It is tied up with Buddhist moral psychology and spiritual aspirations and orientation. It's not just about conduct, it's not just about saying, "You do this or else! If you don't do this then you are going to get this," or "If you do this you will get that kind of reward." It's much subtler and basically comes down to self-cultivation and bringing fulfillment into one's life rather than leading a life guided purely by the idea of what one thinks is right and what one thinks is wrong, thinking that what is right and what is wrong is completely independent of oneself and one's state of mind. It is not the Buddhist view that one's conduct must conform to an external, objectively existing moral order or something like that. This seems to be an important point.

Nagarjuna's Letter begins by discussing the *six reminders* and the importance of what is known as the Triple Gem in Buddhism, namely Buddha, Dharma, and Sangha. The remaining three reminders have to do with the practice itself. Once one begins to think of the Triple Gem as being one's guide, one has to remind oneself of the practice and this is related to the practice of generosity, moral precepts, and contemplation. Contemplation was discussed as being the attainment of divine mind or it is sometimes referred to as "*divine abode*[8]." This was followed by further elaboration on the practices in terms of generosity and moral precepts and the discussion of the six paramitas of Mahayana.

The succeeding section of the text goes into these practices in more detail and includes the practice of meditation. The next verse begins by discussing what laypeople should do and how they should practice. Since this letter was addressed to a king, the verses switch back and forth between advice or counsel for ordained Sangha members and for the non-ordained lay practitioners, such as the king himself.

Filial Piety

Respect and cherish one's father and mother.
This endeavor aligns with a spiritual life and pristine conduct.
Such an approach can permeate one's attitude and conduct toward others
Elevating the mind to a higher realm.

It is very important not to just practice meditation. One needs to ensure that the meditation one practices is aimed towards transforming the mind, and is supported by a proper lifestyle and wholesome livelihood so that one is living well. For a layperson, one needs to think about how to relate to each other; how to relate to other people. How one relates in one's relationships and interactions with other human beings is of paramount importance in terms of the quality of life one will have, whether one has an enriching and reassuring life or one bereft of any feeling of connection, with feelings of loneliness and rejection. That being the case, one should think about those individuals who are near and dear.

A fundamental thing about human beings is that everyone wants to be respected and thought well of by others. This includes those who are near and dear such as one's parents, siblings, and friends. A Buddhist practitioner also has to give some thought to this as a general background and as providing a support system for one's other practices. Therefore, it is important to have a genuine and proper relationship with one's parents or siblings or friends. This basically means we expect varieties of things from them, yet we may not be as forthcoming in terms of the expectations that we have in return. As a friend, brother, sister, daughter, or whomever, one should use this opportunity to learn to develop an affinity with other human beings. The same kind of attitude one may develop with near and dear ones could gradually extend to others, to people who we may have fewer dealings with or people who are not necessarily close or dear to us. Nagarjuna has said that if we do this, it will provide a genuine foundation for all of one's relationships with all beings, including those that we may look up to or seek guidance and counsel from.

The basic point of this verse seems to be that one would be able to utilize this experience to enrich one's dealings with other human beings as well, if we are able to form genuine close relationships with those people that we should have a close relationship with, including one's spouse, children, and so on. In doing this, we can have tangible results in this life. It is a good thing to get along with people we should be getting along with or those we have very tiring and trying relationships with, if we are to look at it from a worldly perspective. From a spiritual point of view this will also be a very healthy thing to have and it will help in the end.

Taking Precepts from Time to Time

> *To strengthen and purify the mind avoid killing,*
> *Theft, sexual misconduct, lying, excessive alcohol,*
> *Overeating, self elevation, aggrandizement,*
> *And all types of excessive indulgences.*

This particular verse is about observing precepts. In the context of moral precepts, when laypeople come to Buddhist teachings and practices they may want to practice generosity and moral precepts, but unlike the monks or nuns who have the leisure to practice these things full-time, a layperson does not have that kind of time available. Therefore, laypeople can take precepts just for the day. As mentioned previously, if one has problems with certain habits and they have become a great source of trouble for us, we can take a precept just for the day. One could take a single precept not to kill for that day or not to lie or whatever the case might be. This verse suggests one could then take more precepts if one wished to. One could take the precept not to kill or to lie or to sleep with one's partner for that day or not to indulge in mind-altering substances. One could also take a precept in terms of the consumption of food. For example, one could say to oneself, "I will only eat vegetarian food today," or one could say, "I will settle for just one meal or I will have two meals a day and skip dinner," or whatever the case might be. This could include the portion size also or how much one is going to eat for that day. For example, one could also not participate in entertainment for that day, such as not going singing and dancing.

Observing these kinds of precepts is a very good way to modify one's habit patterns. Instead of having a very black and white attitude toward those things that are upsetting and thinking either, "I have to stop doing this at all," or "I won't worry about it." The idea is that if we do take these precepts from time to time, then over a long period this will have a cumulative effect. One's behavior will become modified so that the craving for certain things, the strong pull that certain things may present to the person, will begin to diminish. It is also said that it is good to sleep or sit on the floor instead of sitting on high, elevated seating. As one begins to practice in this way then one is able to exercise some power or liberty regarding one's actions. Even if one is still enslaved to certain impulses or tendencies or deep-seated habit patterns and may have a hard time giving them up, nevertheless, taking these precepts does cause interruptions in these patterns. When we are able to refrain from eating more than twice a day or when we do not lie for a day, when one has the cognizance that one is able to actually stop doing these things, this gives an added sense of confidence to the individual. This is how the layperson could learn to practice the aspect of moral precepts so that one can bring about change in how one lives one's life.

At this point somebody might say that the list of behavior that one could take precepts to counter does not include business transactions or the exchange of money or even the handling of goods such as gold. This is already prohibited in the precepts of the novice monk, *sramanera*, (in Sanskrit), "*dge tshul*" (in Tibetan), or novice nun (*sramanerika, dge tshul ma*). According to Nagarjuna, this is allowed for laypeople. It is okay to participate in business transactions and exchange money, as a layperson has to make a living and provide for one's family. On the other hand, a novice monk or nun is not allowed to do this because they have renounced the householder lifestyle and so there is the issue of compatibility there. To handle money is compatible with the layperson that is trying to observe precepts for a day or more but it is not compatible for someone who has taken the novice precepts of the sramanera. It is prohibited for the novice monk or nun because to hoard money and other items such as gold, which are worth a lot of money, is not compatible with trying to simplify life and not have too many possessions.

There is one other question that arises regarding the layperson that is going to take a precept or several precepts for a day or more and the novice monk or nun. The novice monk or nun is the closest in the monastic order to the layperson that has taken precepts. This vow has to do with the precept of not singing, dancing, playing musical instruments, and putting on makeup or perfume for both the novice and the layperson taking precepts for a day or more. In the monastic rules, these precepts are listed as being of two separate kinds. In other words, singing and dancing is one kind of violation and putting on perfume and makeup is another kind of violation. In the case of a layperson this is mentioned as just one violation instead of two. The reason for this is if a layperson violates more than one precept such as taking the vow or precept of not singing or dancing but then goes ahead and does it, according to the instructions one has to make an acknowledgement of this. The violation is counted as only one because for a layperson to violate these precepts is not as grave as for somebody who has taken on robes. So there are differences of that nature which one has to understand. Sramanera is the novice vow and *upavasatha* (in Sanskrit) is the lay precept and there are differences between taking these two kinds of precepts. Even a novice is in a different category to that of the layperson who has taken a precept just for a day or so.

The notion of taking a precept for a day or two is called "*poshadha*" in Sanskrit and "*so jong*" (*gso sbyong*) in Tibetan; "*so*" means restoration and "jong" means to purify or to train. This means when one is observing these precepts, then one is doing two things: one is restoring one's wholesomeness and secondly, one is getting rid of whatever undesirable thing one is trying to overcome. It is just like taking medicine: it has the dual function of reducing and eliminating illness and restoring one's health. As a layperson one can take these kinds of precepts. One may think, "I should not do this," or "I should not say these things," or "I should not be like this," but it is very difficult to stop doing these things. It is very difficult to just switch from being one kind of person to another kind of person. It is less difficult to take a precept for a short period of time and try to exercise restraint.

As discussed previously, refraining from certain behaviors has a cumulative effect just as a continuous drop of water dripping into a bucket soon fills the bucket. It has also been pointed out in other Mahayana literature that the soft landing of water on a rock for a long period of time causes an indentation in the rock. All these examples are given as encouragement to laypeople to do whatever it is that one wishes to do, to just do it. Even if it is not very much and or even if it is for very long, then one should give it a go. If one does this intermittently from time to time over the course of years, then one will become transformed.

Transforming One's Attitude

Forsake disruptive attitudes of miserliness, deceit, hostility,
Laziness, pride, excessive attachment to material things,
Attachment to beauty and youth, sexual attachment,
Excessive desire for power. These distract from a spiritual life.

So far what has been discussed concerns what we can do to change our behavior, bring about some behavioral modification, and what might be the most skillful way to do that. This has to be done in conjunction with a change of attitude and so transforming one's attitude is the point of the verse. These may be attitudes such as miserliness, insincerity, deception, laziness, conceit, haughtiness, excessive attachment to material things, hostility, being proud of one's station in life, of one's physical beauty, of one's education, or to do with having youth or power. Nagarjuna says that a layperson should learn to become conscious of these things within oneself. Miserliness, hostility, haughtiness, and all these things cause disruption and discontentment in one's life. Even if one is feeling very proud, these feelings are still ephemeral and do not last. As long as there is an extreme sense of competitiveness and one is always measuring oneself against others, then one will continue to remain dissatisfied and discontented.

Therefore, one's attention is being diverted from more important things to less important things. These things are some of the most enduring sources of distraction for the individual. All these conflicting emotions are interrelated, and they encourage each other to flourish. Due to miserliness, anger would arise and along with miserliness one would feel the need to deceive, cheat, or misrepresent oneself. These forms of negative emotion have a way of feeding on each other and feeding each other. The individual needs to become aware of these things within oneself so that one can bring about a change in one's outlook if one is serious about leading a good life that is in accordance with the dharmic path. Conceit and pride and so on may give temporary comfort to the individual, but it does not last because one always feels threatened that somebody else might come along who is physically more beautiful or educated or refined, or who is younger or has more power and things of that kind. If one is to follow the Dharmic path, it is possible to excel. It is always possible to learn to better oneself, which is what the dharmic path is all about, while also finding the motivation to be free from unwholesome mental attitudes. It is possible for one to advance, to become better, and to excel without having to be driven by miserliness, covetousness, the use of deceptive tactics, the dissemination of misleading information, misrepresenting oneself to be something that one is not, or projecting the persona of somebody with great qualities and attributes.

The practice of heedfulness is another virtue one needs to think about from time to time. To do that one should think about the next verses:

Practicing Heedfulness

The Buddha said that heedfulness is the source of becoming fully conscious
And heedlessness is the source of darkness and disturbances.
Encourage positive and virtuous mind states
By devotedly applying heedfulness.

Unvirtuous lapses into heedless darkness
Can be reformed to heedful radiance—
As did Nanda, Angulimala, Ajatashatru, and Udayana—
Like the sight of the moon as it appears from behind the clouds.

In order to become conscious of these things we need to practice heedfulness or mindfulness and have self-understanding. It is essential to understand oneself, as we will feel more comfortable with ourselves without being caught up with all the unhelpful disturbing emotions. It will be possible for us to begin to mature and flourish. What will really help us at the end is the flourishing of virtuous qualities. This will make us feel good about and have a sense of appreciation for ourselves. Feelings of conceit and excessive pride are really counterfeit versions. That superficial inflated sense of one's self-importance cannot match what one becomes as one is transformed. As Nagarjuna states, it is like the moon emerging out of the clouds. One begins to glow and shine and such a person will become radiant.

For these reasons one has to practice mindfulness, which helps us both overcome negative states of mind and negative propensities and develop the positive counterparts. When we are heedless we leave ourselves open to all the assaults of emotional afflictions and that brings death to us. If we practice mindfulness, if we are heedful, we become impervious to the assault that we experience from the upsurge of disturbing states of mind. Another thing that we need to realize is the power of habit is very strong, as we already know. If we can recognize the power of negative habits, then why should we not also have similar confidence in the positive habits that we can learn to habituate ourselves to both physically and mentally? We can habituate ourselves to doing those things that we should be doing and thinking while also not doing other things that we should not be wasting time on. What we become habituated to becomes easy. Just as we do not have to think about doing something harmful, in a similar way, the more we do what is helpful the more it will then become second nature to us.

There is nothing that does not become easier from repetition. If we use mindfulness and do these kinds of practices, through habituation one will find it easier to do the things that we are supposed to be doing. It is not about feeling that one should be performing these things out of obligation or duty. One has to understand the soundness of the counsel and then apply them and become habituated to them. Sometimes at the beginning we try our best to habituate ourselves and for a while we can do it. Then a disruption occurs because we have met somebody or some disruptive thing happens in our lives and we discontinue it and revert to our old habits. One may feel that there is no possibility of redeeming what has occurred and then think about the recidivist nature of some of our efforts to overcome old unhelpful habits. Nagarjuna says we should not worry too much about that either and that is not a source for feelings of discouragement. This is to be expected and it is not something that should not be happening. When we have an old, deep-seated negative habit and we are trying to graft a new, more helpful habit pattern onto it, it is not as strong so therefore, the old habits may reassert themselves with some ferocity. The key thing is to persist and not give in and adopt the defeatist attitude.

As has been said in the Buddhist literature, Nanda, Angulimala, Ajatashatru, and Udayana—these are all people who have had lapses. Nanda was Shakyamuni Buddha's half-brother and he was a very lustful kind of person. Even though he tried his best, nevertheless he had a few lapses and with Buddha's help was able to come to his senses. According to another story, Angulimala, which means "one with a garland of fingers," fell under the spell of a very bad teacher. The teacher taught violence as the ultimate thing and if one could feel no qualms about killing and could kill without reservation, this was the most excellent thing that one could aspire to. So Angulimala proceeded to kill a lot of people. One day he saw the Buddha walking along in the distance and wanted to kill him as well. Through their encounter, Angulimala became transformed and gave up his violent ways, again not without some difficulty. Ajatashatru also fell in with bad company and became a friend of Devadatta who was the "fall guy," so to speak, in many of the Buddhist sutras. Under his influence, he committed patricide by killing his own father. His father was a very good man, a king, a Dharmarajah as a matter of fact, and a very spiritually minded ruler. Ajatashatru met up with the Buddha and became transformed even after murdering his own father. He in fact became one of the most advanced disciples of the Buddha at the time. Udayana was a very bad character. He had killed his mother because his mother prohibited him from continuing his lustful nocturnal escapades. When she told him to stop that kind of behavior, he flew into a rage and killed her. He then became completely remorseful and became a monk. He did not tell anyone that he had killed his mother but this was discovered after some time. When the Sangha realized that he had committed matricide he was expelled. He continued with his practice, became reformed, and after a while set up a place for other monks and nuns to come and practice and as a result he became a very highly developed human being.

Many different stories of this nature are told in Mahayana sutras to illustrate the point that bad habits are hard to overcome but simply because they are hard does not mean that they will not get easier to overcome or that they cannot be overcome completely. So, this is another thing that one has to think about.

Apart from being mindful, we also need to practice patience. This is emphasized in the next verse.

The Practice of Patience

A great ascetic practice is that of patience,
Giving anger less opportunity to arise.
The Buddha said overcoming anger
Will secure elevated states of being.

The reason why we do not develop very well is because we feel frustrated—we have such an overwhelming feeling of frustration that it becomes impossible for us to remain focused and feel energized. This comes from having deep-seated anger at oneself and at others. The only remedy for that is to practice patience. Patience means having the courage and fortitude to face difficulties and not expect everything to be smooth sailing. Otherwise whenever some little thing happens or there is a small upset, we think of it as being catastrophic. It becomes the most catastrophic thing and the most amazing disaster that has happened. Nagarjuna says that many other religions speak about penance and the importance of engaging in rigorous ascetic practices where one puts oneself through very arduous physical punishment. Some try to burn themselves with fire, some use water to freeze the body and punish it that way, and others discard normal clothing and wrap themselves in leaves.

Nagarjuna says that these things are useless practices and this is an irony that exists. Many individuals do not fear putting themselves through these life-threatening exercises for the sake of religion or spirituality or for some other reason. However, whenever certain things happen to us, even something as small as somebody saying something nasty or when we hear that somebody has been gossiping about us or some little thing that happens to upset our equilibrium, we immediately feel enraged. We do not have any capacity to deal with disruptions in our lives. If we really want to progress with our lives, one of the things we need to do is learn to work with these disruptions without flying into a rage and crying out in frustration and impotent rage.

According to Nagarjuna, with frustrated rage and anger one feels more and more confined and restricted and the feeling of rage will become even more intense. If one can practice patience, "*kshanti*" (Skt.) or "*zo pa*" (*bzod pa*) in Tibetan, we will not be so timid in terms of facing certain difficulties in life. If there are fluctuations in the course of living, then we will not be thrown about in such a violent way that we feel confused and disoriented so that we have lost all sense of balance or confidence and are left only with rage. Therefore, it is very important not to allow the things that are going on in our lives to get to us in too much of a negative way. We do not have the power to control our environment completely. We cannot instill thoughts in other people's minds with the use of our power, and we cannot force others to behave in certain ways towards us. One needs to adopt a different approach. Instead of reacting to things, one has to learn to respond by adopting more skillful methods so that we do not feel overwhelmed.

In this way, the notion of the practice of kshanti is important. It is described as being like wearing armor if one really uses kshanti properly. Things will not get to us so much and we will not feel so hurt or so put down or humiliated. In that way, we will be able to keep ourselves from sliding back into what are called lower forms of existence or degraded states where negative emotions are rampant with feelings of dejection, lack of appreciation, and depression. These are the things that we need to think about when we want to follow the dharmic path. It is important to approach it in that way so that we have an integrated approach to Buddhist practice, where all aspects of our being are brought to bear in our effort to gain liberation from samsaric existence.

To reiterate, it is important to think about taking moral precepts even if they are for a short time. If relapses occur, it is very helpful not to get discouraged and allow that to make us feel incompetent or not capable of doing anything about it. We are to take heart that if there is some sense of relapse, as long as one is practicing and doing one's best, one is always going forward. When one feels that there is some kind of impasse, this is one of the stages of the path to one's full self-realization. Also, it is useful to think about the importance of learning to handle difficult circumstances and situations and doing this in a very gradual manner by being skillful. First one practices in relation to less disturbing things and then gradually one uses that to deal with more disturbing and upsetting experiences in life.

The Buddhist view is that if we have the right attitude, then that same attitude can be used to deal with varieties of disturbing states of mind and different adverse circumstances and situations. As discussed previously, it is about capacity and this has to do with the strengthening of one's habit, which in some Buddhist literature is called the planting of white seeds. This means that if we have a helpful thought or emotion or attitude, we do not underestimate its importance. It is like a seed that will germinate and take root so that little thoughts and emotions can grow into something very powerful, something that can have a big impact. We know this to be true with negative thoughts and we have to realize that is also the case with positive thoughts. If the negative thought of suspicion or lack of trust can turn into full-blown paranoia then similarly, if we could be thinking about something helpful even though that might last only for a short time, this will be very beneficial.

As it is said in *Bodhicaryavatara* by Shantideva, it is "like a flash of lightning on a dark night where for a split second the path has been illuminated." If it is like that, nevertheless the imprint is made; it is etched in the recesses of our mind and with further cultivation it will germinate and grow. Therefore, one should not be thinking, "I am either patient or impatient." Patience is something that one has to cultivate and get used to. As it becomes part of one's repertoire of how one approaches life and how one interacts with others and deals with situations, this will become part of one's nature. These are some of the fundamental things that one needs to think about when one wants to practice Buddhist teachings.

The practice of patience is also very important with regard to the creation of negative karma. To reiterate, negative karma was previously discussed as it relates to the object, the affliction, the intention, the preparation, and the completion. One needs to be clear that all of those things have to be present. The object of karma has to be present along with the intent or intention, which has two components. First is the conception, which is to have cognizance of the object. Secondly, the motivation to do harm that is fueled by negative thoughts and emotions needs to be present. The preparation has to be present and this has to do with the use of what are called the three gates of body, speech, and mind. The emotional affliction has to be present and finally the act has to be consummated. Even if all the other things are present but the act is not consummated, which means there is no loss of life or loss of property or something like that, then the karmic action has not been completed. Some karma has been created, but it is not complete. Sometimes there may be loss of life but still it may not be a full-blown negative karmic act because the intention was not present, or the object was mistaken or misconceived, or strong emotion was not there, or something may have been stolen but one didn't intend to steal it. It is evident that karma is quite complex and this is something that needs to be understood. Sometimes in the West it is thought of in a very linear kind of way: that you do this act and something bad happens and then you have to suffer the consequence of that negative action. It may not be as straightforward as that. To qualify as a real negative karmic act, we need to assume that all the other factors are present.

Preparation for Meditation—Counsel to Laypeople

Nagarjuna continues the Letter by setting out the counsel to laypeople in nine key points. The first point is the importance of filial piety and of being able to get along with the people with whom we are supposed to be getting along, even before we make new friendships or establish new relationships. It is important to cultivate a sense of rapport with people who are near and dear to us and to have mutual respect.

The second point is about the importance of taking precepts from time to time and doing that for a day or more. Nagarjuna reiterates points he has made earlier concerning the importance of taking precepts. The precepts are called "*nyen ne*" (*bsnyan gnas*) in Tibetan, or "*upavasah*" in Sanskrit. Whatever one wants to refrain from doing or if there are certain habit patterns that one wishes to curb, one should take precepts that work against them and practice "*posadha*." For example, one tries not to utter angry words for the day or do anything else that one thinks one has problems with. The taking of the precept is called "*posadha*" (in Sanskrit) or "*so jong*" in Tibetan. "*So jong*" has the connotation of both purification and restoration.

The third point is about the change of attitude. In addition to taking the precepts on a fairly regular basis, one should learn to change one's attitude. It is not just about learning how to curb certain physical and verbal activities. This learning has to be supported by a change of attitude such as trying not to be too covetous and learning how to have self-knowledge in terms of things that are troublesome to the mind.

The fourth point is about the practice of mindfulness and it is something that one has to exercise. Mindfulness here should really be called heedfulness, because "*bag yo*" (*bag yod*) means heedfulness and mindfulness is called "*dran pa*." "*Dran pa*" or mindfulness is like the species and "*bag yo*" or heedfulness is like the genera, if that is the correct expression. Another way to understand it is that the word heedfulness encompasses mindfulness, but mindfulness does not encompass heedfulness. Heedfulness is helpful in order to practice the precepts and to gain more insight into oneself. As previously stated regarding the practice of precepts, sometimes we may practice heedfulness and we may try to do our best with the precepts and get a grip on ourselves by becoming more conscious of ourselves generally, and with our different states of mind more specifically. Nevertheless, we may not be satisfied with what we have been able to do and we may feel stuck or that we are going backwards and have relapsed. We should not feel too discouraged when these things happen. We should never think that our efforts are not going to bear fruit. We should not allow ourselves to be too discouraged. The point being that if we apply heedfulness this will also help. The more we allow our mind to go on a rampage of self-condemnation and into very negative frames of mind or become overly critical of things, the more we become heedless. If we are heedful we might be able to maintain a positive frame of mind and not allow the negativities to take over.

The fifth point is we should apply patience or *kshanti*. Nagarjuna states that this is the most important ascetic practice one can do. Often religious people think that putting oneself through very severe penance is the best form of ascetic practice. In Buddhism, learning to deal with day-to-day upsets and difficulties, ranging from little irritating things to big catastrophes, and how we handle ourselves in those situations determines whether we are capable of exercising kshanti or not. This is the main thing and trying to deliberately put oneself through extreme hardship is not the point. The point is how we deal with the things that happen to us.

Giving up Enmity

> *"If abused and defeated by others and*
> *Having things stolen from you"*
> *Leaves you argumentative and resentful*
> *Skillful use of patience defuses enmity, then one can rest happily.*

This verse is also devoted to patience. If we can exercise patience in the right way, in a skillful and in a wholesome way, we will become less irritable and less easily provoked. This is a very important part of leading a happy life. The more that things get to us, then the more irritated we become and the more irritated we become, then the more enraged we become. The irritation will build up and this turns into rage, rage turns into an impotent form of rage and one's sense of frustration becomes heightened. As it is explained in Mahayana teachings, through the use of kshanti we should learn not to be like this, although it may still happen that we get upset or angry. We may try to practice patience or kshanti in a skillful manner but we cannot help it: we still get upset. Nagarjuna states that when this happens, the remedy is to at least try not to harbor enmity or resentment. We may be angry because we think somebody has said something derogatory about us, or somebody has stolen something from us or taken advantage of us or put us down and denigrated us. When these kinds of thoughts are formed in our mind, of course one is upset at that point, but we still have a choice. We can keep dwelling on it, getting more and more upset and more and more resentful, or we can just get upset and then get on with it, move on and not carry that around. According to Nagarjuna, somebody who gets upset but is able to gradually let go would even be able to have a good night's sleep, whereas somebody who is unable to let go cannot even have a good night's sleep because they are reliving the whole thing over and over, over and over. What happens is one begins to add more and more elements to the story and everything becomes more and more elaborate, and then it is not even about what actually took place. Even if one has become angry and thinking that so-and-so has said this about me or so-and-so was being very physically aggressive towards me or as the commentary says, even if somebody has hit us and there was a physical struggle involved, if these things have happened, the important thing is not to allow them to take hold of our mind and occupy our mind completely.

As Shantideva has said in *Bodhicaryavatara*[9], whenever there is a sense of resentment or bitterness, this leaves a bitter taste in our mouth and we can never have enjoyment. Even if we are doing something enjoyable, a nagging feeling is always there depriving us of the opportunity to enjoy the things we are doing that we would normally find enjoyable. By thinking about these things, one should think that being resentful does not serve any purpose. If it were useful in some way, of course there would be no point in trying to overcome it but being resentful does not serve any purpose. One is unable to redress the harm done and it only exacerbates the harm that has already been done.

The sixth point concerns learning how to abandon a way of living that is harmful and degrading to us, based on our body, speech, and mind. How should we try to live well? What is living well as opposed to not living well? This is explained in the next verse.

To Practice Correct Conduct of Body, Speech, and Mind

Recognize mind's impressions are like etching in water,
earth, or stone.
The first of mind's tendencies of water and earth
Will help those possessing defilements
And the final for those strong in positive mind.

Nagarjuna says that our mind works in very different ways. Sometimes our mind is very stubborn and inflexible and sometimes it is very flippant and does not stick or persist with anything. Mind has these two tendencies: it is either very stable and does not move or it is very flexible and moving all the time. These things can also happen at the same time where part of the mind remains the same and another part is constantly changing. According to Nagarjuna, we should make use of both of these tendencies as a lay practitioner. As mentioned previously, we should not allow the mind to latch on to resentment and bitterness and things of that kind and should let them go. This is like trying to draw something on the surface of moving water. If we try to draw on the surface of water, it will not work. Similarly, when things impact on our mind and if it is something that we find offensive, hurtful, or upsetting then we should not harbor or dwell on that too much. We should try to let go and forget it as much as we can. If that is not possible, then we should not let it linger on too long. Even if we think about it for a while, we should eventually let it go and not allow it to take hold so that we do not become a very bitter person at the end. It can often happen that being bitter becomes part of a person's character and their way of being and this is how one begins to relate to everything and everyone. These impressions should be allowed to be like a drawing on sand or dirt: they will remain for a while but the weather will take care of it. They are completely erased.

Similarly, after a while we should have the ability to let go of whatever negative impressions the mind carries by no longer thinking about them: not thinking about who has done what and who has said what. One has forgotten the incident, whatever that might have been. When we receive positive impressions, we should do what we used to do with our negative tendencies. These we should try to hang on to, hold on to, so they become stabilized. These impressions should be turned into carvings on the face of a rock that will have endurance. It will endure all kinds of weather changes and the impact of the rain and sun and storms.

When positive impressions are made in the mind, they should be cared for in a similar fashion. As the changing wind of circumstance comes about, we should make sure that those impressions have not been erased because of the sudden changes in the environment or in one's personal experiences. We should use that part of our mind that latches on and retains things to strengthen the positive experiences, and that aspect of the mind that is very feeble, fickle, and unreliable for the negative impressions, so that one can let go. It is not good when we forget all the good things that we have done or experienced and only remember the bad things: it should be the opposite. We should try to get on with life and not let the past negative experiences haunt us any longer.

The meaning of this particular verse is that the positive experiences and impressions should be made stronger like etchings on a hard surface. This is part of the sixth point regarding how to train the body, speech, and mind of the individual.

The Importance of Pleasant Speech

The Buddha declared that pleasant, truthful, and wrong
Are three kinds of speech.
Words are like honey, flowers, and filth.
Abandon the last one.

This verse deals with the notion of speech. Three different kinds of speech are discussed: pleasant speech, truthful speech, and wrongful speech. We have to learn to speak properly. We have spoken about the mind in terms of how we should make use of it in terms of its flexibility or its inflexible nature. How human beings interact with others is based upon communication and the primary form of communication is conducted through the use of speech. Although we make many different kinds of use of speech, according to the teachings they are grouped into three.

1. The first one is called pleasant speech, which means saying encouraging things that others would like to hear. For example, trying to inspire others or saying things that are supportive of somebody. That is something that one should do. Pleasant speech has the impact of making others happy so what one has said makes somebody happy. In the teachings this is compared to a taste of honey.

2. The second one is truthful speech, which means to say something with sincerity. "Truthful" means something that is said not in terms of words but in terms of sincere speech and that means being sincere about what one is saying. When saying something pleasant to somebody, one should say it with sincerity. For example, flattery may not be considered pleasant speech even though it may be seen as something that is pleasant for somebody to hear. Sincere speech is said to be very beautiful—there is some kind of beauty in what is said with sincerity and it moves people. It has a very beneficial impact on others.

3. Wrongful speech is the opposite of these two. It is saying things in order to hurt others or to make them feel upset, to demean them or to put them down, or it is saying things without sincerity to deceive and manipulate. Nagarjuna

says that the third form of speech is something that one should avoid and one should try to practice the other two forms of speech as much as possible.

Whatever is said makes an impact on the minds of others. Others will remember if one has said something nice to them. Therefore, even in terms of practicality one will receive a positive response or positive feedback from others. If we have said something very hurtful or demeaning, then others will respond in a similar fashion and one would then feel angered or demeaned or humiliated. From the Buddhist point of view, we have to look at this in terms of interpersonal impact: how what one says impacts upon others and how that then impacts upon us. We should then think about the migratory nature of sentient creatures.

The Four Forms of Migration

The four directions a migrating person can move,
From: light to extreme light; darkness to extreme darkness;
Light to extreme darkness; and dark to extreme light.
Migrate in the direction of the first.

Sentient beings are migratory beings: they are never stationary for very long and when they move, they move in different ways. They can move from light to light or from darkness to darkness or from darkness to light or from light to darkness. Four forms of migration are spoken about in Buddhist teachings.

- Moving from light to light means that because of what we have done in the past as sentient beings our future is assured. It looks good that we move from light to light and there is a smooth transition that we can make in terms of where we are going. Our future looks promising.
- Another scenario could be that one is going from darkness to darkness, according to what we have been and what we

have done. In this instance, we have been totally negligent in regard to our thoughts and behavior. We have been stumbling around in the dark with no direction and we may be headed that way in the future so the same thing may be in store for us.

- Moving from darkness to light is the third possibility. In this scenario, even though we have come from darkness we may suddenly get some kind of impetus or inspiration to become more self-reflective. We may be able to move into the area of light by thinking that we have been wasting time and fumbling around in the dark and now we want to lead a more conscious and purposeful life.
- The other option is we may have been good but we have become more negligent and as we deteriorate we descend into darkness. What we need to do is try to at least move from darkness to light. If we are fortunate enough to be moving from light to light that is a tremendous blessing. If not, we should not move from light to darkness. At the very least we should try to make the effort to come out of darkness and into light.

In this particular context, light and darkness means the light of wisdom and insight, and the darkness of ignorance. As long as we do not reflect on our lives and continue to move along based upon our impulses and deep habits, then we are going to be fumbling in the dark. Through effort and the inculcation of spiritual practices in the way that has been laid out in this text, one could move from the darkness of ignorance into the light of wisdom. Furthermore, in the future one should have the resolve to move from light to light and not entertain the thought of moving from light into darkness again. This means one should not lose courage, despair, or give up hope, as mentioned earlier, but always think about how one has taken on the dharmic path. One then has the capacity to continue on that journey.

The seventh point is about companionship and the sort of company one should keep.

The Four Categories of Persons

> *Human beings can be understood to be like mango fruits:*
> *Unripened yet appear ripe; ripened yet appear unripe;*
> *Unripened and appear unripe;*
> *Ripened and appear to be ripe.*

It goes without saying that human beings are very varied in their complexity. Normally they can be grouped into four different categories. If we use the mango as an example there are four different types:

The mango that is not ripe inside but from the outside looks ripe
The mango that is ripe inside but from the outside looks unripe
The mango that is unripe inside and outside
The mango that is ripe both inside and outside

Human beings are very similar. Some human beings are not ripe inside but are ripe on the outside and others are ripe inside, but not ripe outside. Then there are those who are not ripe either outside or inside and those who are ripe both outside and inside. This means that some people may be a bit nasty but they come across as being very nice and people who are actually quite nice inside who come across as being very unpleasant. Some people are unpleasant full stop—both unpleasant inside and unpleasant on the outside—and then there are people who are pleasant both inside and outside. When one is choosing one's friends one should think about this carefully, trying to show some discernment regarding the character of one's friends. Of course, if somebody is nice both inside and outside, there is no problem. Somebody may not come across as very nice but in fact may be a very nice person, so that is the kind of friend one may wish to have. Somebody who is not very nice but comes across as being nice one may want to avoid, even though that person behaves as though they are different from what they actually are. The person who is not really nice, who has deep character flaws and behaves in a very obnoxious manner has to be avoided. Nagarjuna's point is that unless we already have a very strong character, then we are very easily influenced by others. It is very easy to fall under the influence of negativity if we do not surround ourselves with friends who can be supportive in the right way. Therefore, the choice of friends is an important part of how to lead a good life.

At least initially, from these four different types of friends there are two that one can mix with and two that one may wish to avoid. This is also put into context because if one advances on the path and practices the bodhisattva way of life, then one tries to extend oneself to all and sundry, depending on one's capacity. At the beginning if one is feeling a bit vulnerable and easily influenced, the choice of friends is a very important part of one's practice.

This discussion has covered seven of the nine points that Nagarjuna mentions regarding the practice of a layperson.

So far Nagarjuna has been speaking about the importance of things such as going from darkness into light or if one is not going from light to light, then at least ensuring that one does not go from darkness into darkness or from light into darkness. It is important as one begins to mature and grow older that one has more wisdom. When one is younger, if one shows intelligence but neglects that and begins to become deteriorated, then one is not doing justice to oneself.

In a similar way, if one is mixing with the wrong people and is unable to associate with many people whose outward behavior and character coincide completely, nevertheless we can be with people who have good character but whose behavior may be a bit rough on the edges. If possible, we should try to find people who have good character and are also an example to one in terms of how to interact with other people. We draw inspiration from these people. As a Buddhist practitioner we should try to think about these things.

Refraining From Causing Harm to Others

> *Avoid pursuing another's wife.*
> *However she appears think of her differently*
> *As mother, daughter, or sister.*
> *If lust persists, meditate on impurities within the body beneath the skin.*

As a layperson or an ordinary person who is unordained, sexual relationships in themselves are not regarded as being harmful. However, if one interferes with the relationship of a married couple this may bring about all kinds of unexpected and undesirable consequences. Therefore, by thinking about all the things that could be disruptive and painful for several people, one should try to discourage lustful tendencies directed towards somebody's wife, for example. As it is said in the sutras, in such circumstances one should try to think of the woman in a different way. If the woman is older, one may want to think of that woman as one's mother, if that woman is within one's age group, then one might want to think of her as one's sister, and if she is younger, one may want to think of her as one's daughter. One could use these kinds of techniques in order to curb one's sexual desire for others wives. Trying to change one's attitude by trying to see the other person in a different way should help. Nagarjuna says that one should not gaze at the woman that one is attracted to, giving her longing and lingering looks, otherwise it encourages the feeling even more. Therefore, it is best not to gaze too much and when not doing that, one should try to think about that woman as described.

Sometimes even if one is by oneself, the image of the person appears. One cannot get that person out of one's mind and the sexual longing still arises in a very intense fashion. Nagarjuna says that one could analyze and dissect that image; "go underneath the skin." If one thinks of that person in terms of the skeletal frame and the skin, the nervous system, and the organs, then this could help curb the sexual desire that one is feeling. By extension, one could do this with inanimate objects such as a house that one is attracted to, or whatever the case might be. In other words, when the visual impression is so strong and one is only seeing the surface, then the attraction is tremendous. When one begins to analyze, dissect, and deconstruct that image, this should also have a positive and beneficial effect in the form of giving some relief. That is something that one also needs to think about in terms of the object of one's desire. One has to think about whether the object of desire is appropriate or not. Some objects of desire may bring about our own ruin and harm to others as well, unless we do something about it. As it is explained, some of these situations can cause a volatile environment and so tremendous harm may be spread around. The other thing one needs to do is to really pay attention to one's mind. How one's mind is behaving, how the mind is chasing after various sensory objects and latching on to things is something that one needs to be constantly aware of. Therefore, guarding and protecting the mind is very important in this respect as well.

Protecting the Mind

Protect the unsteady swaying mind as you would protect your
Accumulated knowledge, progeny, a precious jewel, or life itself.
Withdraw the mind from sense disturbances as you would protect yourself
From an agitated snake, poison, a weapon, enemy, or fire.

According to Nagarjuna, we should think of the mind as being extremely precious and quite fragile because it is easily swayed. In this way, the mind also needs some kind of strength training in the form of willpower. Weakness of will means that one is easily swayed and does not have a lot of control, so we can increase our willpower by protecting the mind. Nagarjuna says that we should protect it as being extremely precious. For example, it would be a tremendous tragedy if we had learnt something through the course of our life that we really cherish and would really feel the loss of, but then found we no longer had any memory of as a result of memory loss. We should think of the mind in the same fashion. Without the mind we would be incapable of doing anything, attaining anything, or growing and maturing. The mind should be protected like life itself or like a precious jewel. Even though it is the mind that experiences suffering, nevertheless it is also that same mind that affords us so much joy and pleasure in life. We should try to discard all the sources that would harm that precious thing, just as we would not want to handle a poisonous snake because the poison is life-threatening, or handle explosives because we might blow ourselves up or lose a limb or body parts in the process—meaning that we would be suffering for the rest of our lives.

We should avoid all that is harmful to the mind just as we would like to avoid our enemies, because our enemies would try to cause disturbances in our lives. We should try to avoid them like we would avoid wildfire. We would try to put it out because otherwise the fire would consume everything in its path. In this way, we have to think of all the things that are harmful to the mind and then try to protect the mind from those harmful sources.

The next verse explains how one might go about doing this at the beginning and how to protect the mind from these harmful effects.

Uprooting the Cause of Excessive Desire

The Lord Buddha declared excessive desires to be like the
Champaka fruit, as they are the cause of misery.
The iron chains of these excesses bind beings to the prison of
samsara.
Renounce them.

Excessive desire is at the root of our problems because our desires are too numerous to be satisfied. We come to recognize this fact and we realize that there is no way that all the desires we experience can be satisfied. This is the number one realization that we must have. When we do not understand this and when our desires are not satisfied, then frustration, anger, and resentment set in. The other thing that one should realize is the limited satisfaction of desires in the normal context. Unless we are trying to satisfy desires in the way that is set out in the teachings in this text for example, then the satisfaction we feel is going to last only for a given period of time. It is not long-lasting even if that desire is satisfied. There are a number of points we can consider in relation to working with excessive desire.

1. Firstly, many desires will never be satisfied.
2. Of those desires that can be satisfied, we do not realize that even if we are able to satisfy them, on one level they will still not be satisfied because dissatisfaction will arise again. We have to then keep on satisfying our desires over and over.
3. Thirdly, we have to realize that for those two fundamental reasons we have to put our desire into perspective because otherwise we will continue to experience suffering. Our mind will then become weakened because it is too busy trying to scramble after everything that one finds desirable or alluring or seductive.

4. The fourth point is that of all the normal forms of desire that we experience, the objects of desire do not last. They do not give lasting satisfaction because they are like the champaka fruit, which has a nice appearance but is very horrible inside. The pleasure that one gets from eating fruit like this lasts only for a short time.

Therefore, the wise person knows how to deal with desire in the proper manner so that the individual does not end up like an ant or a moth. Ants, being attracted to honey, become stuck to the substance in their endeavor to savor the taste. Moths are killed by throwing themselves into the flickering flames. Unless we know how to handle desire and distinguish the different forms of desire from each other and the appropriate objects of desire from non-appropriate ones, we will be like ants and moths. It will bring ruin to us because of our weakness of will that causes us to chase after everything. As has been said, there are many desires we cannot satisfy and even the ones that we can satisfy remain unfulfilled in the end. Instead, they may bring ruin to oneself, as would excessive indulgence in substances or substance abuse. This is another way to think about protecting the mind.

Mastering the Six Sense Organs

To choose between the one who conquers attachment
Of momentary distractions apprehended by the six sense organs
And the one who conquers armies in battle,
The wise knows the first to be the far greater hero.

We also need to consider the way in which the six sense organs are related to the different states of mind and to the disturbance or lack of disturbance in the mind. Nagarjuna says one has become a true victor, a true warrior, if one is able to deal with sensory impressions in the proper manner and use the sensory organs for one's own benefit, rather than just following them. One is able to exercise one's sense of autonomy and willpower so that the sensory impressions are utilized for one's own benefit. If we yield to the sensory impressions in an indiscriminate fashion without any kind of sensibility whatsoever and just follow our senses, we become de-centered and are unable to overcome the turbulence. One is like a warrior when one does not fall victim to one's sensory impressions but is able to direct one's focus on sensory inputs in a more directed, managed way. Somebody who engages in a normal battle and wins that battle is not the real warrior. The real hero is the one who does not get beaten down by the onslaught of sensory impressions. The individual is then able to truly enjoy these sensory impressions, as opposed to being completely bombarded and disturbed by all the inputs. This is another way in which one can think of protecting the mind.

Abandoning Excessive Desires

Just as lepers disturbed by their sores
Use fire for temporary relief,
Excessive clinging to desires
Brings no peace.

Somebody who suffers from leprosy scratches all the time because they are covered in sores and the sores are very, very itchy. They keep scratching them, which only makes it worse. Sometimes in order to get some relief, they try to expose the sores to fire and that brings about some relief but only for a short time. In the long term, this exacerbates the condition even more. Nagarjuna says if we are not skilled in learning how to direct and manage our desires, then we are no better than this proverbial leprosy sufferer because we will keep doing the same thing over and over without realizing it.

In other words, just by doing more of the same with the many desires that we experience does not bring about more satisfaction. In fact, doing more only reinforces the habit and the pleasure becomes decreased. In this way, in repeating whatever we are used to finding pleasurable over and over again, the habitual behavior becomes stronger and stronger. Even if we do more and more of whatever that pleasurable thing is, the satisfaction and pleasure it affords decreases in proportion to the increase in effort that is put into it. Therefore, it becomes a self-defeating task. This point is something one should also think about in terms of how to cement our willpower so that we do not suffer from weakness of will but can untangle ourselves from these deep-seated habits.

Nagarjuna says that these are just methods and temporary measures. These are all just techniques that we may use in order to deal with weakness of will—from the technique of looking at another's wife as a mother or sister, down to the example of leprosy. As has been said, this comes from learning how to manage our desires properly—not aiming towards the eradication of desires but learning how to channel and manage desires better. The way in which we can really deal with our desires is to have some understanding and some insight into reality. This will help us to manage our desires properly in the ultimate sense.

The Development of Wisdom

The Nature of Reality

What has been discussed so far in terms of handling our desire is related to the skillful use of methods and how to work with them. How to see reality so that we have a different understanding of things even in relation to sensory objects is subsequently considered in the text.

Meditation on Dependent Origination

Be skilled in perceiving things as they are
Through understanding Ultimate Truth.
There is no other contemplation to practice
That possesses comparable quality than this.

Understanding ultimate truth is the best way to work with our desire. If we try to gain insight into reality, then we will have some understanding of the sensory objects, the physical objects, audile objects, nasal objects, and tactile objects. When we say ultimate truth, what we mean is getting to know something about how things exist in reality, rather than how things appear to us. Everything exists dependent on each other. Nagarjuna's main work on emptiness *Mulamadhyamika-karika* states that it is not something that we can understand because somebody else can point it out to us or something that we can understand through the use of our normal intellect. It is something that one can understand by oneself through the development of what is called discriminating wisdom. We have to try to understand interdependent arising if we want to understand the reality of things. Even at an early stage, if we understand interdependent arising, then we will have some intimation or inkling of what ultimate reality might be.

All the different religious founders and philosophers have spoken about some kind of "supreme being" or some kind of metaphysical substance that is responsible for the continuation and maintenance of the world as we know it. However, if we understand interdependent arising, we will see that this sort of explanation is not tenable. According to Nagarjuna, it is due to not understanding interdependent arising that we have been drawn into a deep state of ignorance. Therefore, very strong passions and disturbing emotions arise. It is also because of this that we have a very strong sense of an individual self that exists in isolation or even in opposition to everything else that exists. From this, all different kinds of notions of self and other come about which then go towards inflaming conflicting emotions. When one looks at an object for example, the object is objectified, and one thinks of oneself as being separate and dissociated from the object perceived—there is a thought that there is a physical object or a physical form that I'm looking at. With this kind of dualistic notion, the emotions are aroused. Not only are emotions aroused, but varieties of conceptual confusion are also created through this mistaken notion. If we have some understanding of interdependent arising, then we will understand that self and other are relational concepts: not only are they concepts, but self and other are almost relational things; they are interdependent. If we understand interdependent arising, then all different kinds of dualistic notions will begin to subside.

Therefore, if one thinks there are separate entities in terms of subject and object or self and other, it becomes evident that this understanding is not based in reality. It is only our consciousness objectifying the sensory object as being something out there, existing independently of the subjective mind. This does not suggest that subject and object are identical or the same. Rather, it should be understood, that subject and object are interdependently arising and that both subject and object arise equally due to causes and conditions. This means there is no primacy position accorded either to the object or the subject. The subject does not have any supervenience over the object or visa-versa.

According to the Buddhist view, when we say that things arise due to causes and conditions, it means things come into being because of varieties of causes and conditions. There is a whole assembly of causes and conditions and there is no linear history or causal chain to be traced. In this way, when the appropriate causes and conditions congregate at an appropriate time and place, things come into being. When the causes and conditions that would perpetuate or sustain the duration or existence of that particular entity—whatever that might be—are not present, then that particular entity would cease to exist and disintegrate.

From the Buddhist point of view, if we contemplate and meditate on this properly, we will begin to see things and even sensory objects in a different way. It will follow suit that if we see things in a different way, our responses to those things will also be different. One is still making use of the sensory apparatuses and still able to have sensory experiences, appropriate emotions, feelings, and to conceptualize what one is experiencing. How one experiences these things changes if one has gained some insight into the notion of interdependent arising. From this point of view, the notion of interdependent arising is used in Mahayana Buddhism to bridge what we call the relative truth and the absolute truth. The absolute truth represents how things exist and the relative truth represents how things appear to us. Through an understanding of interdependent arising we can gain insight into both and this is called the "middle view" in Mahayana Buddhism. If one does not maintain the middle view from an understanding of interdependent arising, then one could fall into the extreme of simply thinking of an absolute reality at the expense of relative reality, or one could fall into the extreme of relative reality and ignore the existence of ultimate reality.

The concept of interdependent arising shows us both how things exist in themselves, and how things appear to us. To understand this, we need a new faculty called *prajna* or discriminating wisdom, which is cultivated through contemplation and meditation on interdependent arising and emptiness. Meditation on interdependent arising and emptiness and the cultivation of prajna are the real antidotes to our disturbed mind, and that will allow us to clear up our delusional notions about the sensory inputs.

In the next verse, Nagarjuna emphasizes both the importance of a sound ethical basis and the importance of wisdom, which were briefly discussed in the previous section. There has to be a balance between the two. The basic point is that someone who is following the Buddhist path properly has to embody both of these qualities. One needs to embody ethical goodness and the power of wisdom.

Cultivating the Superior Qualities

The person possessing a high birth, beauty, and good education
Will not attract respect if they lack wisdom and ethical conduct.
One who possesses these two qualities
Even though lacking the others will be highly esteemed.

Sometimes it is useful to make the distinction between what is understood by morality and the understanding of ethics. Ethics concerns how we are to lead our life, and how to live well, and morality is concerned with not lying or stealing and things of this nature. Therefore, morality has to do with following the rules. As discussed previously, amongst the six paramitas are the virtues of generosity, patience, and vigor, as well as "*shila*"—sometimes translated as morality, sometimes as ethics and translated as moral precepts or morality in the context of this discussion. "*Shila*" (Skt.) in this instance is like morality, whereas all the others are the ethical values one needs to cultivate. We cannot say somebody should be patient just in the same way that we can say that somebody should not lie or kill.

According to Nagarjuna, somebody who possesses the ethical qualities is a very superior being if they are also endowed with wisdom. People normally admire somebody who comes from a good family, who has good breeding, very attractive features, and is also very educated and sophisticated. Nagarjuna states this is true to an extent. If somebody does not come from a very good family, is not particularly attractive, or does not possess any of these qualities but does possess the goodness of ethical qualities and wisdom, then that kind of person is to be admired. Furthermore, Nagarjuna states that if somebody possesses these two qualities, one could even be devoid of the other qualities and that would not matter very much; this is even recognized by most ordinary people. If one were to ask most people what sort of person they admire and respect—either a person who has good breeding, is highly educated, who and is very handsome and charming, or someone who has wisdom and possesses the goodness of ethical qualities—most would choose the second kind.

Such a person is truly admirable, according to Nagarjuna. They would not be compelled or tempted to do something harmful to themselves or others, as this person possesses ethical goodness. The individual would have an inclination or propensity to do something beneficial for themselves and others due to possessing wisdom. Though admirable, possessing any of the other qualities does not make one ethical, and will not stop somebody from doing something harmful, either to oneself or others or from failing to do what is beneficial and a source of happiness and joy both for oneself and others. Somebody who pursues these two forms of excellence is called an *Aryan* in Sanskrit and "*che bu dampa*" (*skye bu dam pa*) in Tibetan, which means becoming an elevated or superior type of being. In the next verse Nagarjuna gives counsel regarding how to refrain from getting caught up in what are called the "*eight worldly dharmas*" in Buddhism.

Regarding the Eight Worldly Dharmas Equally

> *The Eight Worldly Dharmas—gain and loss, pleasure and pain,*
> *pleasant words and unpleasant words, praise and blame—*
> *View them equally.*
> *These should not consume your mind.*

In Tibetan "*jik ten cho je*" (*jig rten chos brgyad*) means the "*eight worldly dharmas.*" According to Nagarjuna, while we are in this world, everything that we do is governed by these. The word "*dharmas*" in this particular context means something like factors, so they could also be termed the eight worldly factors. The first pair is gain and loss, the second pair consists of pleasure and pain, the third pair consists of praise and blame, and the fourth pair is what is pleasant to hear and unpleasant to hear, or pleasant things said about one and unpleasant things said about one. We care about these things a lot. We think of one side of the sets or pairs to be something that we need to have and the other side of the pairs to be something to be free of, to be rid of.

To elaborate further, Nagarjuna says:

> We all want to gain, we all want success, we want to get ahead, we want more things—that is what we want. Any kind of loss that we suffer is terrible: when we lose our properties and when we lose friends.
>
> We want our life to be full of pleasure and we do not want pain so we seek pleasure wherever we can find it; we look for it and we avoid pain at all costs.
>
> We want people to say nice things about us; we do not want people gossiping about us behind our backs.
>
> We want people to praise us; we do not want them to put us down or say derogatory things about us.

Nagarjuna states that we have to be careful in terms of how we understand these sets of factors. We should not think the "*eight worldly dharmas*" means that we should not have them or that we should go out of our way not to gain anything, or not think that being praised is better than being denigrated. It means that we should not look for them too much and we should not care too much whether people are praising us or putting us down or that one wants any kind of pain. It also means that we should be able to handle losses when they occur and not be thrown into a deep state of depression or despair. As Nagarjuna states, even highly advanced spiritual people still experience all of these things. They may experience gain, praise, and all of these things. They are not shunned; it does not mean that one has to shun them. What it does mean is that one should not be obsessed about going overboard in terms of trying to have more wealth and more properties or trying to make sure that people are praising us and not denigrating us. This is another thing that a Buddhist practitioner should try to find a balance with. Being in the world, we cannot avoid them. Again, it is about attitude; it is how we handle the "*eight worldly dharmas*" that determines whether we are going to lead a good life or a bad one.

Consequences of Negative Karma Cannot be Shared

Refrain from harmful acts to satisfy Brahamanic superiors,
Monastics, deities, parents, siblings, royalty, ministers,
or attendants,
Because there is no way
To share the fruits of your own negative karma.

Nagarjuna states that there are many different kinds of people who follow different religious paths and some may preach violence and death. If somebody who is serious about the Buddhist path comes across someone who preaches this sort of thing they should not take any notice. There cannot be a Brahman, monk, or even a god, king, queen, ministers, or people in power who could actually make one do these things, pretending they are good or that it is a religious duty to kill. If we believe in karma, then whatever deed one performs, only oneself bears the consequences of one's actions. This is not something that one can share with the co-conspirators. When someone performs a grievous deed and the consequences of the act are not immediately apparent, sometimes we may think the negative karma associated with the act is not very significant, but this is not accurate. Karma basically ripens in three different ways. Sometimes a karmic act fructifies or bears fruit fairly immediately in a short time frame. Others are delayed somewhat and there are yet others that do not bear fruit for quite a long time. This depends on the surrounding circumstances and situations and the weight of the karma that has been created. Nagarjuna says one should realize that killing or anything of that kind is not something that one can justify in the name of spiritual practice.

The Action of Karma

> *Harmful behavior performed*
> *May not wound you immediately like a weapon.*
> *Results arising from harmful actions will manifest*
> *Eventually, at the time of death, after, or before.*

If we have done something that is karmically unsavory or unwholesome, we may not immediately suffer any kind of ill effect from that action. It is not like a knife cutting through our flesh; there might not be an immediate visible or tangible feeling experienced following from what one has done. Nevertheless, if we really have done something quite horrendous, most people have some conscience. Nagarjuna says even though they may suppress it for many years, when the time of death arrives suddenly the individual will remember all the things that one has done and be completely gripped by regret. Just because we do not immediately feel something bad or experience any adverse effect from having committed some ill-conceived karmic deed, we should not then shirk our responsibility and say, "Well it doesn't really matter." Even in this life we may later on come to regret it, but once something has been done it is very difficult to undo. It is better not to do something to begin with. If one has any doubt that one might regret the action, for example, even if it is before dying, then it is important to consider why we would go ahead and do it with the lingering suspicion that later on one may be traumatized by the actions one has taken. Nagarjuna says that even though we know that we may not immediately feel anything untoward, we should try not to do those things that we have any doubts about.

According to Nagarjuna, if we really want to enrich ourselves, feel confident, and have a good sense of self-worth, then doing all the negative or harmful things that we have discussed is not the right way to go about it. The right way to go about building a healthy sense of self-esteem is to amass the wealth of The Noble Ones. There are seven means suggested in the text to amass this kind of wealth.

Acquiring the Wealth of the Holy Ones

The Buddha said that trust, ethical standing, extending oneself generously,
Building knowledge and understanding, humility, self review, regard for others,
And wisdom are the seven properties of the elevated being.
Recognize other common properties to be meaningless.

Firstly, Nagarjuna says that in order to amass this kind of wealth, we have to have some trust. If we are always suspicious and untrusting, then it is very difficult to develop rapport with others. It is also very difficult to develop rapport with the Buddha and the Dharma. One may doubt the veracity of the Buddha's words or even the reality or existence of the enlightened state and always be mistrustful of others motives, of others intentions, and be projecting all kinds of things onto others. One does not feel comfortable thinking this way and this is not a good place to be in, so one should have some kind of trust.

Secondly, one needs to have a sense of decorum and conscientiousness. One needs to do the right thing and not be "all over the place," but have stable principles that one lives by.

The third type of wealth is to forgo a poverty-stricken mentality, which is being covetous and miserly and try to develop a more generous disposition and demeanor. It is not only about giving material things away, but also how one extends oneself to others both in terms of physical action and the words uttered. When one does not feel as poverty-stricken, that lifts up one's spirit and one has a good feeling about oneself.

The fourth type of wealth one should accumulate concerns learning. It is very important to exercise and stimulate one's mind and broaden one's knowledge so one will have a better sense of oneself. The fifth type of wealth is not to hide too many of our shortcomings because if we are too secretive, then paranoia sets in and one is engulfed in self-doubt and a sense of uncertainty regarding oneself. So, it is very important to learn to let go of things and break clean of one's past attachments.

We need to realize that it is okay to feel embarrassed if there is a good reason to be embarrassed about something one has done. It is not a bad thing to feel embarrassed when it is appropriate to have that response. In fact, being totally reckless and having no regard for oneself and others causes one to have a diminished attitude towards oneself.

The last type of wealth discussed is to have a general sense of how others are going to feel about certain things in terms of one's actions or speech. Before one acts rashly, one needs to have given some thought to what impact it might have on others, how they may respond, and whether they are going to be angry or resentful or upset or whatever the case might be. Having some sensitivity in relation to the attitudes of others towards one's behavior is also an important thing, because if others begin to form a bad judgment about the character of an individual, then that individual is going to suffer from all sorts of self-doubt and develop self-demeaning attitudes.

These are the Seven Treasures: trust, a sense of ethical standing, generosity, learning, trying to be beyond reproach, having some kind of shame or feeling of embarrassment, and having sensitivity towards others. They are called the "Seven Treasures of the Aryas," the elevated beings. Nagarjuna says if we cultivate these seven treasures, not only would this go a long way towards making our spiritual growth faster, but even how our life is lived normally would be altered. Everything that is said here regarding what we need to do applies in our normal circumstances. If we do these things, we will get on better with other people, be seen in a better light by others, and it is the right thing to do. Nagarjuna states that it is true that to have a huge stash of money or gold or whatever is a good thing and that represents wealth, but the real wealth has to be within. One does not become rich simply because of what a person possesses, what a person has. One becomes rich from what one is. At the end, whether a person is going to feel good about themselves is not dependent on what one has or possesses. Instead, it depends on what one believes one is, knowing that there is good reason to feel good about oneself because one has put in the riches that one needs in order to flourish. Knowing that, then one becomes a genuinely richly endowed person. Nagarjuna clearly emphasizes the importance of enriching oneself within and not just focusing on the external wealth. Amassing a lot of external wealth is not the only or the best way to make oneself rich; rather, the best way to enrich oneself is through self-cultivation. It is the sort of person one is that is the important consideration and not what a person owns or has.

That being said, the next couple of verses or stanzas are devoted to describing how one should try to preserve that wealth and not let it diminish.

Preserving Inner Wealth

Avoid indulging in the six that result in loss of good character
And lead to diminished states: gambling, seeking endless entertainment,
Laziness, keeping poor company, excessive alcohol consumption,
And mischievousness at night.

According to Nagarjuna, we have to protect the *seven treasures*. When we try to accumulate this wealth, we should also guard it like we would guard normal material possessions, or whatever we accumulate is wasted. One of the main avenues through which we may squander this wealth comes from being heedless and engaging in reckless behavior. We also pick up all kinds of addictive behaviors such as gambling, alcohol consumption, becoming totally absorbed in entertainments of all kinds, singing, dancing, going out all night and then sleeping all day, whiling away the time, and just having a good time. Engaging in these behaviors does tremendous damage to the possibility of being able to make something of oneself. Even if one has the intention and from time to time makes some effort in the way described earlier, if these things become part of one's life and most of the time is spent gambling or partying or getting drunk, one will squander whatever has been accumulated. Therefore, it is very important to be aware of these things and not do them in excess.

Being a layperson, one is not restricted from engaging in any of these things at all, but rather, one should not do them in such a way that this leads to a total state of heedlessness and recklessness. As Nagarjuna says, if one continues to behave in this way, not only do we suffer in terms of being deprived of an opportunity to become a full person, but even in terms of worldly standards of behavior, we will be ridiculed or made fun of by others. Due to a gambling addiction or a fondness for alcohol and so on, people might call one a "drunk" or some such thing. Therefore, from both a worldly and a trans-worldly point of view, it is not good to indulge too much in these things because this will go towards making the chance of losing the *seven treasures* greater.

The next verse describes the best way to preserve this wealth.

The Importance of Contentment

> *The Buddha has said*
> *Satisfaction is the best of all riches*
> *Learn to appreciate. If content*
> *Even if one has little wealth, one is truly rich.*

The way to preserve one's inner wealth is not to be obsessive about the pursuit of external things and to learn to appreciate and enjoy things more. One does not think that the enjoyment is only in the accumulation, but it is important that one feels a sense of satisfaction and enjoyment in what one has, in what one is experiencing. One picks up the art of how to enjoy life, the things that one has, from sensory experiences to what one is drinking, eating, doing, and so on. If we learn to derive enjoyment from doing even little things and experiencing different things about life, this adds to the richness of our life. If we are always discontented and frustrated, then no matter how much we are able to accumulate, we are totally unhappy and still feel deprived and poor. One is always feeling poor, so it is difficult to enjoy what one has and there is no satisfaction. Gaining satisfaction from our varied experiences is one of the ways in which we can learn to preserve the riches within us. As Nagarjuna says, to be able to do that, even if one does not have very much, one is enjoying everything that is experienced. Some people are able to do this. So, we should think about this also.

The Importance of Having Few Desires

> *Gracious King, just as the most excellent of Nagas*
> *Suffers according to the number of heads to protect,*
> *So one suffers if dissatisfaction persists while possessions acquired rise.*
> *Less suffering is experienced with fewer desires.*

As mentioned previously, Nagarjuna says that if we allow more and more desires to go unchecked and let unbridled desires proliferate, this only adds to our misery and in any case, many of the desires cannot be satisfied even from a practical point of view. What is more, because we do not know how to enjoy what we have, then more things will mean more worry and more anxiety. More things mean more worry rather than less worry. In other words, the amassing of wealth is not commensurate with the level of satisfaction one gets. There is no connection between the two. Greater wealth does not mean greater satisfaction; in fact, it might be that one is less satisfied. As Nagarjuna says, whether one feels satisfied or not is an attitude of the mind. It has to come from how one is seeing and approaching one's life. If one does not have the right approach, then having and accumulating more things simply means having more headaches. As the Indian mythological story has it, there are many naga kings, "naga kings" being kings of the underworld, and the more powerful they are, the more heads they have. The story goes that there are opportunists who covet the nagas' heads. As nagas are supposed to be surrounded by riches, they also have very ornate headgear, so more heads mean more precious stones. The headhunters so to speak, try to get to the nagas, so the nagas with the most heads have the most to protect and the most worry. In a similar way, the more things we have and the more wealth we have spread around, the more things we have to worry about. When we do not have the right attitude, our worries will increase.

Therefore, the point is whether one has had wealth before and does not have it now, or one does not have it now but one is thinking of having wealth in the future, or one has wealth now, regardless, one should have the same kind of attitude. If one has had wealth before but one does not have it now, then one should not let oneself feel forlorn and depressed and completely lost. If one wants to create wealth, then one should not be so greedy and reckless in its pursuit. If one has wealth already, then one should have a sense of appreciation of things. This is another way in which a layperson could be thinking in order lead a better and richer life.

This concludes the section on how to lead a proper life as a layperson.

The Practice of Meditation

The next part of the text is devoted to providing counsel for both laypeople and ordained people. The first verse is devoted to the way in which we should do our formal practice of meditation regarding our attitude toward food.

Cultivating Tranquility

Understand food to be like medicine.
Use it with neither anger nor aversion,
Nor greed, pride, or beauty,
But solely for maintaining a healthy body.

When we want to do formal practice like meditation, it is not just a mental exercise, as meditation has to be supported by the body. This means that we need to pay attention even to what we are eating, how we are eating, and with what attitude we are eating. This is especially important when we are doing meditation as an intensive practice every day and we have a program. One should try to have the right attitude at mealtimes when eating food at a specific time of day or night. The attitude one should have is to view food as being medicine, something that is nourishing and good for one. Another consideration is the manner of eating. The food itself is viewed as medicine and the manner in which one eats that food has to be devoid of greed and aversion. Greed means gobbling things up and eating in a very fast way. It is important not to eat with hatred and this means not to use food as a means, thinking of food as only being good for the body. For example, one makes an effort not to think, "If I eat this or that food, my physique will improve or I will have more strength." This is seen as showing some element of aggression. One should avoid these two modes of eating. The next thing one should think about is the portion, which has to do with not eating too much or too little. Particularly when we are meditating, it has an almost immediate impact depending on whether we are meditating on an empty stomach or a full stomach. If we think about these things in terms of how to view food and the manner of eating, the purpose of eating is actually to have a healthy body so that one can utilize it for a greater purpose.

It is not just for the body to get stronger, but someone with a healthy body is able to do a lot of things that a sick person would have difficulty with. If one has health, then one is able to meditate better and that should be the purpose. The purpose is to have a healthy body so that one can make use of it for a higher goal, rather than simply to make the body itself better. One should be thinking about those things: how to view food, the manner of eating, the portion, the quality of the food, and the purpose for which one is eating that food. Having the right kind of approach even with food can create a healthy condition to practice meditation.

Meditate Before Sleep and Upon Waking

Oh Righteous one, devoting your day to intensive meditation practice,
At the beginning and end of slumber
Be conscious and mindful then sleep peacefully
So even the time of sleep will bear positive fruit.

These two points in the stanza should be thought of when we are practicing meditation day and night in an intensive way, such as in a retreat environment when we arise in the morning and when we go to sleep. Conscious sleeping and conscious awakening are of paramount importance. One sleeps only during the middle period but as one begins to fall asleep and as one begins to rouse from sleep one should try to be conscious. It is important not to go to sleep in a bad mood or thinking disturbing thoughts or worrying about something or other, or waking up and immediately having something disturbing in one's mind. If thoughts like these arise, one should try to calm them and give oneself positive feedback by thinking, "I will make good use of today and will do my best to utilize the time properly." When one goes to sleep, one should think about sleeping in a quiet and peaceful manner. In this way, even sleep itself becomes something useful. One can utilize it properly instead of seeing sleep as a way of becoming completely unconscious.

As the Buddha has said, when one is going to sleep one could try lying on one's right side with the left leg on top of the right leg and the right hand resting underneath one's head on the pillow. This could also be tried to add more mindfulness to our way of sleeping. In Buddhist literature, this posture of sleeping is called the "lion posture" where the right hand is placed lying under the head and the left foot is resting straight on the right foot. At least in the beginning, the idea is that whether for a few seconds or a few minutes, one is using sleeping-time as an opportunity to adopt some kind of posture and not just letting one's body go and becoming unconscious. These are some of the preliminary things that one could be doing to help one's meditation improve. Nagarjuna also states that one of the practices one could do is the practice of loving-kindness, which is one of the meditations of the "four immeasurables."

The Four Immeasurables

Always contemplate with right attitude upon immeasurable
Love, compassion, joy, and equanimity.

Even if the enlightened state is not gained through these contemplations,
Still elevated and expansive loving-kindness will be attained.

According to Nagarjuna, the real state of Brahma or Godhead is to practice the loving-kindness meditation of the four immeasurables. When we have immeasurable love, immeasurable compassion, immeasurable joy, and immeasurable equanimity, we are in a divine state. One could think about love, which has to do with the wish that sentient beings meet with all that is pleasurable and with the cause of all the pleasures. Compassion arises from the thought, "May sentient beings be free of suffering and the causes of suffering." Joy arises from the thought that this is possible and has happened, whereby sentient beings have the causes of happiness and pleasure and the causes of the removal of suffering and of the causes of suffering. One meditates in a state of equanimity so that one is able to have a really good, positive feeling generated towards all different kinds of sentient beings. One is thinking about those who are close to one or who one is attracted to, as well as towards all those who may be distant from us or that we may have very strong, intense dislike for.

Unlike real life, one of the advantages of this type of meditation is that through an act of imagination, we can bring love and compassion to everyone and they are transformed, and we are capable of extending that love to numberless sentient creatures. It is called "immeasurable" as one can imagine a great, great number of beings that we may not even meet in real life. When we do this kind of meditation, it is done on three different levels. These levels have to do with blending the love and compassion aspects with wisdom.

The three tiers of this practice consist of meditating on the four immeasurables using ordinary sentient beings as objects of meditation.

(1) The first is called: using sentient beings as the object of the meditation of compassion.
(2) The second: using dharmas or conditioned existence as the object of the meditation of compassion.
(3) The third: the objectless meditation of compassion.

Contemplating the Nature of Appearances

Initially, we think about ordinary sentient beings as they are, as we normally see people. On this first level we are simply looking at how human beings appear and how other sentient beings appear. If we are doing this practice in an intensive environment, we try to get to the next level.

Contemplating Interdependence

On the second level, we think of sentient beings as not being individual, discrete, separate sentient creatures, like a group of billiard balls, but as sentient creatures perceived from the point of view of interdependent arising. We are thinking about sentient beings a little more in the context of seeing how everything is mutually dependent on other things. Instead of, "I am thinking about this sentient creature who is suffering from poverty or from malnutrition or disease," one is trying to look at the interconnected nature of all things. Here, the use of the wisdom element comes in, practiced in a skillful manner so that the feeling of compassion is not diminished.

Contemplating Ultimate Reality

The third point is seeing that all sentient beings are part of the same reality. All sentient beings are permeated by the same reality because ultimate reality does not discriminate: it is all-encompassing. Everything and everyone exists within the sphere of Dharmadhatu, meaning ultimate reality. Contemplating these three aspects simultaneously is the important thing. Simultaneously means that first one thinks of sentient beings as ordinary sentient beings, and then one thinks of their interdependent nature, and then one sees things from the ultimate point of view, going back and forth in this way and seeing that these three perspectives are interrelated. These are not alternative ways of looking at the same thing but are complementary ways of looking at the same reality. Although there is a difference in terms of understanding, all these ways of perceiving reality are legitimate. Somebody who understands Dharmadhatu has attained enlightenment. When we are meditating we should meditate in this way even though it is something we have not yet experienced. We are not just cultivating loving-kindness but are also developing wisdom at the same time. We can see how these two are intimately tied together and not separate. It is not the case that the wisdom aspect is something that is separate from the compassion aspect or that compassion can be divorced from wisdom.

When one is using sentient beings as the object of one's meditation, one should begin by trying to use one's family, friends, and people we care about as objects of this meditation. One should then try to imagine strangers and people we do not know about, but who we know exist, practicing the four immeasurables while thinking about them. Eventually we try to practice these meditations by specifically invoking images of people who we distinctly despise. We practice love and compassion first and then joy, thinking that all these things have happened.

If your friends and family are suffering from specific problems, then you imagine those problems have disappeared, that they have what they want, whether it is health or money, and that they are feeling contented. We do the same practice with strangers and enemies in mind and then we should try to practice "*upeksha*" or equanimity. After having thought about people whom we like and those that we dislike, one then tries to calm oneself and remain in a state of openness, in a generous mode so that one has an accommodating attitude.

The Practice of Shamatha

The next verse is devoted to the description of the practice of shamatha or tranquility meditation and the levels of meditative concentration one can attain through this practice.

The Four Levels of Concentration

> *Having gained insight into the realm of desire and having*
> *Abandoned its excesses by means of the four contemplations,*
> *The divine states of concentration—*
> *Brahma, Abhasvara, Subhakritsna, and Brihatphala—*
> *is obtained.*

Nagarjuna's Letter is basically about the *six reminders*, and the discussion so far has proceeded though the reminders in detail, particularly in relation to the three remaining ones. The last reminder referred to the "divine states" where it was explained that "divine states" refers to levels of meditative attainment. This particular verse explains how these divine states are obtained. These kinds of practices are explained more fully elsewhere. The main point referred to in this verse gives an outline of the types of meditation one should be doing, along with the practice of the *Brahma-vihara* or four immeasurables meditation. One should also do shamatha or tranquility meditation. When one does tranquility meditation one can cultivate various states of meditative concentration.

1. As one begins to practice at the first level, the meditator may use the meditative tools called investigation or examination and analysis. At this point one aims towards

attaining the first level of samadhi or meditative concentration. This comes from attaining what is called the meditative experience of bliss and joy, which is an outcome of gaining one-pointed meditative concentration. It is characterized by these three things, one-pointed meditative concentration, joy, and bliss.

2. As one begins to go further, one no longer uses examination and analysis. One only has the experience of joy and bliss and meditative concentration. The two mental activities of analysis and examination are not present.

3. Through the use of mindfulness and awareness, one begins to attain higher levels of states of equanimity where one ceases to experience meditative joy but the meditative experience of bliss still remains. This is supported by one pointed meditative concentration and is called the third level of samadhi.

4. At the fourth level of samadhi, even the use of mindfulness and awareness are abandoned, as they are no longer necessary. The distinct experience of meditative bliss is not present because one goes into a deep state of meditative absorption. This is characterized by the feeling or *vedana* (vedana means "feeling") of neutrality, which is neither pleasurable nor painful. In Buddhism, the feeling of neutrality is described as being a distinct kind of feeling; it is not the opposite of feeling but a third kind of feeling. This state is of course supported by meditative concentration. This is called the fourth level of samadhi and is seen as being a state of total absorption, a state of absorptiveness.

These four states of samadhi are described as corresponding to the states of the gods, the first with "*Brahma*," the second samadhi with "*Abhasvara*," the third with "*Subhakritsna*," and the fourth one with "*Brihatphala*." The fourth level of concentration or samadhi or meditative concentration itself has three stages: the small, middling, and advanced states of the fourth level samadhi. This is the kind of meditative training that one could engage in, in conjunction with the practice of the four immeasurables through the practice of shamatha.

The next verse is devoted to the notion that simply because we are meditating we should not forget all the things that have been discussed in terms of how to live our lives, how to observe moral precepts, and how to cultivate ethical goodness.

Cultivating Virtues

From the foundation of five great practices—
Persistence, intention, preparation, remedial form,
and corrective action—
Virtuous and non-virtuous aspirations arise.
With vigilance strive to do only virtuous deeds.

Nagarjuna says that sometimes we may believe that if we start to do meditation, then everything will be all right in our lives and will fall into place, but we should not think like this. Even if we are practicing the meditation of the four immeasurables or the meditation of samadhi, we should still think about our ethical conduct. We should try to pursue virtue and overcome vices. Our actions are governed by karma in the form of intention, in the form of preparation, in the form of remedial, corrective actions, and in the form of the object of actions. In terms of intention, we can have an intention that is motivated by positive emotions or negative emotions. Positive emotions will impel us to do something that is beneficial and negative emotions will do the opposite, with the object being an object either of benefit or harm. One should always be very vigilant about these things. We should not neglect our responsibilities and use our meditation practice as an excuse for not doing what we need to do to benefit ourselves and others.

At the beginning it might be difficult not to continue with old habits, as has been explained previously. What one needs to do is try to mix some good with the bad and gradually what is good might overwhelm or overpower the bad.

The Power of Virtue

Adding a small amount of salt changes the taste of a little water
While it would not change that of the great Ganges river.
Similarly, small non-virtuous deeds will not spoil
A vast river of virtue.

The idea here is that if a little salt water is poured into a small container, then the whole container assumes the taste of salt water, but if a small amount of salt water is added to a big volume of non-salt water such as the Ganges, for example, then it has no effect. In this way, we should try to mix something good, some of our virtues with our vices so that the virtues begin to become stronger and the vices begin to become weaker. When the virtues begin to gain sufficient strength, it builds up resistance and even if some vices persist they will have very little adverse effect. Even if one is not completely free of vices, as long as the virtues are there and getting stronger then the ill effects of the vices will diminish in time. Nagarjuna says we must take comfort in that thought. One should think of this as a form of encouragement relating to how one can do things. Even if certain things seem insurmountable, through a skillful approach it is possible to overcome them.

There is also the notion that even if some of our undesirable aspects do not immediately disappear, nevertheless these things will begin to yield and in time will be overcome. One does not need to be too concerned about the remaining unwholesome tendencies that may still linger. One needs to integrate meditation with how one conducts oneself in daily life and have that balance as the best way to go forward. One should not think that leading a good life is the most important thing and that meditation is less important. One should not think, "Why do formal meditation?" or "If I do a lot of meditation I do not really need to worry too much about anything else because after all, meditation is the most important thing." One should try to have some kind of balance. While thinking this way one must continue with the practice of meditation. When we practice meditation, we are trying to overcome negative states of mind. We have all kinds of negativities going on in our mind and in the Buddhist teachings, all of the negative states of mind are grouped into five categories.

The Five Obscurations

> *Be aware that the five meditative obstacles*
> *Are mental states that rob the richness from virtue:*
> *Insolence, harmful thoughts,*
> *Apathetic lethargy, excessive craving, and doubt.*

Nagarjuna states that the obstacles we need to deal with during meditation are the same ones that we have to deal with in everyday life because they also impact upon our behavior.

- The first obstacle is the unruly mind or the mind that is jumping all over the place, scattered and diffused, along with the unhelpful and negative mind of regret, meaning not being able to let go of things, hanging onto things, and wishing things were different.
- The next negative state is the mind of wanting to or drawing pleasure from doing harm to others by thinking that causing harm to others is good for one.
- The next obstacle is the mind that is depressed and filled with apathy, which makes it very unworkable. With

depression and apathy, it also includes sleepiness and lethargy, wanting to sleep. Even though they are a bit different they are nevertheless connected so are listed as one.

- The next negative state is excessive greed, excessive craving and grasping.
- The last one is an extreme form of doubt and uncertainty.

These are described as the five negative states of mind. All the different kinds of negativities that we experience can be grouped under one or the other of these five mental states, which are states that do not allow our mind to operate and function properly. Either our mind is too agitated or it has become dull and inactive and completely stops functioning. These are the other two tendencies that these five have the effect of producing. Either one is feeling very down, low, heavy, lethargic, and sleepy or one is agitated and in a state of heightened anxiety. We do shamatha meditation in order to deal with these different types of mind. The reason why shamatha is practiced is to deal with the effect these negative states have on our behavior. Due to excessive craving and grasping and the feeling of wanting to do harm means these two tendencies make it very difficult for us to follow the moral behavior of not killing, not lying, and not stealing. The lethargic and unserviceable mind has the effect of not being able to direct our actions towards higher goals. One feels discouraged and unable to take any initiative to aim high and think about the possibilities of what one can achieve through one's actions. One does not think about what one can do to make things better. When the mind is diffused and scattered with feelings such as regret, these negative mind-states prevent one from being able to think clearly and exercise intelligence and wisdom regarding one's actions. Through the practice of shamatha meditation and vipashyana or insight meditation, we try to deal with the kinds of disturbing mind that are harmful to one's actions.

In terms of one's day-to-day actions, if one's mind is divided, one becomes incapacitated and can't act because one is always thinking about all kinds of possibilities.

Extreme doubt causes disturbances because when one is meditating, one is always thinking, "What is happening, what's going on and how do I know it works?" and so on and so forth. One does not make any progress because one is unable to give anything a chance, not allowing anything to work either in terms of one's actions or one's practice of meditation. The practice of shamatha meditation is very helpful to deal with these negative states of mind but it has to be supported by insight meditation. Before we do that, we need to think about other kinds of practices we can do to make our meditation better. Nagarjuna says we need to use the five powers at all times to drive us with our practice of meditation and with our actions as well.

The Five Powers

Unremittingly apply the five excellent strengthening practices—
Faith and trust, vigor, mindfulness, concentration, and wisdom.
These are named the five powers when applied,
And the five faculties when attained.

- Faith means that instead of indulging in negative forms of doubt we should try to develop *shraddha* or trust. We have to believe in the workability of certain things. If not, we preempt having any power to operate in a positive way. If we read literature written by meditators, we have to believe that these meditators did experience the things they said they experienced. When they tell us to meditate this way rather than that way, we would be better served if we followed their instructions than if we did not. These are some of the examples of how we may want to cultivate trust.
- The next power is vigor. Always trying to remain interested

in things is extremely important, otherwise we may feel very unmotivated or flat. It is not good for meditation or for doing anything else in life, so one has to have vigor.

- The third power is to practice mindfulness; not just in meditation but in post meditation as well.
- In daily life one tries to focus on what one is doing—even if not all the time and even though it may be difficult. If we try as much as possible to stay with what we are doing through attention and concentration, in that instance, then we are practicing samadhi.
- One has to use wisdom or *prajna*. Whatever *prajna* we may have developed through the practice of vipashyana or insight meditation we should use that in meditation and in daily life.

So these are called the five powers in Buddhism. In Buddhism we have an elaborate description of the paths and stages of a practitioner. At the beginning of one's practice they are called the five powers but later on they are called the five faculties. When one is struggling to practice these, they are termed the five powers and when one has become efficient in their use they are called the five faculties. If we use these five powers, they will have a direct impact on the five disturbing states of mind, so their cultivation helps us to deal with the five negative states of mind listed earlier.

To review the text thus far, Nagarjuna has discussed the distinction between outer and inner wealth and the way in which we can make the distinction in relation to the satisfaction of desires. The discussion has also covered the way in which outer wealth can produce only temporary happiness, whereas inner wealth can produce ultimate happiness. Somebody who has inner wealth can enjoy outer wealth much more whereas somebody who is poor internally, but externally rich or wealthy, is unable to attain real happiness. Real happiness comes from inner enrichment and that comes from cultivating the treasures the teachings speak about. Nagarjuna has also discussed what should be done to protect and preserve those treasures and increase the mass of wealth within. Our inner wealth can be protected through the practice of meditation, and through leading one's life in a more heedful way by modifying one's behavior in terms of not spending too much time in gaming establishments or whiling away our time drinking in bars and so on as a part of one's regular activities. Other ways in which this can be done are to pay attention to the disturbing states of mind and to cultivate the five powers and so on. The use of the five powers is also helpful when one is doing meditation on loving-kindness, shamatha or tranquility meditation, developing various states of concentration, and engaging in insight meditation practice. Therefore, the five powers help to deal with the disturbed mind and with our meditation practice.

The next verse discusses the importance of maintaining a level head and staying grounded. When we do these practices, we may feel as though we are progressing and doing quite well, but even though we think we are making progress, we need to be aware that we are still subject to the sufferings of samsara. Therefore, reflection on the next verse is a useful contemplation.

The Importance of Humility

> *"I have taken birth due to my karma,*
> *I will get old, sick, die, and be separated from those I love."*
> *Arrogance will be arrested and not arise*
> *By repeatedly contemplating in this way.*

We should think: "Because I have taken birth in this world, on many different levels I am just like everybody else. I am subject to the same things as others. I will also get old, I will get sick, I will die. I have to experience those kinds of sufferings like everybody else. I am still subject to karma and whatever I sow I will reap."

Thinking in this way will keep us grounded, which is a very important thing. With the use of the five powers and the practices, even if one is developing as a human being, one has to develop in the right way. Staying grounded is an important part of that growth. If we are going off on a tangent and getting all kinds of weird ideas, we lose touch again. We may not be able to profit as much afterwards from all the gains we may have made. As mentioned, one should try to stay grounded and levelheaded by thinking "I am like everybody else. I will get old and I will get sick." In this way all sentient beings are equal.

Right View

Buddhist practices are concerned with what we should do and this has two components.

1. What we should do, meaning how we should behave through our body and speech.
2. What we should do in terms of our mind, particularly to do with the practice of meditation.

What we need to do in these two instances has to be supported by the right view. If what we do is not guided by the right view, we may get sidetracked and lost. Therefore, the development of the right view is emphasized in the next verse.

Be Guided by Right View

Be guided by the right view
If higher states and liberation are desired.
Even ethically admirable deeds will be corrupted
If the wrong view is maintained.

According to Nagarjuna, there are those of us who follow the Buddhist path that have two different kinds of desires in terms of self-fulfillment, one being a temporary and immediate goal and the other being a more distant, sublime goal. The immediate goal is one whereby we are trying to improve ourselves and lift ourselves up, trying to go forward, to develop and mature and attain higher and higher states of mind and better and better ways to be. The more distant goal is to attain enlightenment. If we have those desires, then we should be doing more than simply engaging in virtuous actions and shamatha or calming meditation. We may try to calm our mind and to engage in sound ethical behavior, but if we have the wrong view, that does not help. Even if we do something ethically admirable it becomes corrupted, so having the right view is important.

In this particular instance, the wrong view could be related to two things. On one level, one might think of ethical behavior as being the most significant thing: that it is what one does that counts. On another level, one may develop the wrong view by thinking that if one is pursuing certain spiritual practices, then one would be free from acting in a responsible fashion. In other words, one would not have to do anything to benefit oneself and others because one would be beyond the pale of ethical standards of goodness. These kinds of wrong views could arise and so one has to try not to have wrong views.

In order to understand what the right view is we have to think about things in the following manner, which is connected to vipashyana or insight meditation.

The Four Seals

> *The reality should be known that human beings are*
> *Dissatisfied, impermanent, lack a selfhood, and are filled*
> *with disclarity.*

> *Lack of mindful application leads to disrepair*
> *Through misapprehending these four.*

What one needs to do to develop the right view at the beginning concerns the following points:

> To realize that everything is impermanent. We have to have a real grasp of this fact in terms of both our internal experiences and mental states, and in terms of the external world and what goes on around us.
>
> To realize that even though we may think that there is an unchanging self to be found, there is no such self found upon investigation.
>
> Owing to the fact that what we think of as being permanent is impermanent and because there is no self, one has to come to recognize that these are impure perceptions. Understanding these things will set the stage for the development of proper view. The proper view is explained in more detail in the next couple of verses.

The Nature of The Self and Aggregates

> *Thus has been said: the body is not the self;*
> *The self is not the body; the self does not dwell in the body;*
> *The body does not dwell in the self.*
> *In this way, see the four remaining aggregates as insubstantial.*

In Buddhism the self is thought of as being a collection of aggregates and *skandhas*, which means that not any one of the skandhas or aggregates can be identified as the self. We have some notion of the self when the aggregates come together. This is the basis of the designation or imputation of the notion of the self. When we say aggregates, we are talking about the notion that the self consists of physical and mental elements. Both the physical and mental elements have to be present for any kind of recognition of self to occur. In considering the relationship between the physical body and the self, one might ask:

"Is the self the same as the physical body or is the self different from the physical body?"

Nagarjuna states that either answer would be incorrect. If we said that the self was the same as the physical body, this answer would be wrong. If we said that the self and the physical body were separate, this too would be wrong. The reason is that when we think about the self we think of it as being something that remains fixed and unchanged. We may think, "My body grows and a lot of changes occur in my body but my self is the witness that stands apart from all that is happening. The self itself is not being changed thereby, despite the bodily changes occurring, the least of which might involve the aging process itself." So, if we said that the self and the body were the same, we would have to say that is not true. When the body changed, the self would also have to change, so then the self and the body would not be separate. Therefore, the self cannot be a witness and remain aloof and stand by and observe all of these changes occurring in the body because the self would not be separate from the body.

Nagarjuna says that if the body and the self were completely identical, then whatever happened to the body should happen to the self. That is not the case because things can happen to the body but the self is not affected in the same way as the body. The self experiences things differently, even if the same things are occurring to the body. If the self and the body were identical, when things happened to the body, in the same way, the self should have the same experiences occurring. Therefore, if the same thing happens to the body, if it is affected in the same way on two separate occasions, for varieties of reasons the self will experience things differently. Many examples like this can be presented which suggests that the self and the body are not completely identical because the self has conscious experiences that often contradict the indications of physical change. Therefore, the body and self are not separate or the same. Nagarjuna says we should think about the self and the different aspects of the mind in the same way, in terms of the aggregates. As part of the aggregates, we speak about feeling, disposition, consciousness, and perceptual experiences but Nagarjuna states that we cannot even identify the self with consciousness or with feelings, so therefore the self is not identical with feelings nor is it separate.

Through this series of reflections, we may engage in analysis regarding what the self is, and we will come to the realization that the self is not identical with the psychophysical constituents or separate from them. In Buddhism and according to Nagarjuna, this is because the self, like everything else, is not a simple unified concept. With all the various elements coming together we have some kind of experience of a self but if there were no aggregates, no psychophysical constituents, there would be no notion of a self. It is in this way one should think of the self. We should not think of the psychophysical constituents as the basis and the self as something attached to those psychophysical constituents as a dependent entity, as this is also not true. The self should also not be thought of as the basis upon which the psychophysical constituents attach themselves. In other words, we should not think that the psychophysical constituents are there and because of that, this self is there as something separate but dependent upon the psychophysical constituents. Nor should we think that the self is primary because the psychophysical constituents arise as contingent phenomena based on the pre-existing self. Therefore, we should not think either that the self is dependent on the psychophysical constituents or that the psychophysical constituents are based on the self. Nagarjuna says this is a very important thing to think about and one should spend time meditating on these things as part of one's vipashyana meditation.

As part of vipashyana meditation we have two tasks in front of us. One is to have some kind of understanding of the self. The other is to understand the self in relation to the world, which is the way one should understand the world itself. The meditation should begin with the self and then proceed onto meditation on one's relationship to the world. When we are doing this meditation on the skandhas and the self, one should not think this means there is no self, that one has to go to the realization that there is no self at all. That should not be the outcome of this meditation. The other point is that one should not conclude there is some kind of self or soul as an unchanging, permanent psychic entity that we can find apart from the various functions of the consciousness and our bodily elements and states. This is called "the middle view" in Buddhism, which is not to latch onto some kind of metaphysical concept of the self or soul or to deny that there is any kind of self at all. On the empirical level, there is a bearer of moral responsibilities that is responsible for ethical engagement, so there is an agent and a bearer of the fruit of the deeds performed. The only thing that is being said is that we have a strong tendency to think of the self as some kind of inner governor or director who directs all the operations while not being involved in any of the operations itself. That kind of notion is being denied. As long as the aggregates persist, there is an agent and there are actions being performed and one experiences the relevant emotions and experiences arising from one's interactions with the world, and as the fruit of one's deeds.

After reflecting on these meditations—one should learn from other sources where they are presented in more detail—one should go into the meditation on the world and one's relationship to the world. The main thing that one needs to contemplate is how the world comes to be the way it is and how one happens to be in this world. Nagarjuna says that one should try to limit one's speculative enquiry. The reason for this is explained in more depth further on in the text. To begin with, we need to think about how the world happens to be the way it is. The world happens to be here not through some kind of fortuitous circumstance or just by chance with no rhyme or reason. Nor has the world been created for us or designed or fashioned by some superior being that remains outside of that created world. Nagarjuna states that we need to look into these points and try to develop the correct view through the practice of vipashyana meditation.

The Nature of Conditioned Existence

> *Know this, the aggregates do not originate from*
> *Chance, time, nature,*
> *Intrinsically, metaphysically, or without causation*
> *But manifest through samsaric activity and craving.*

According to Nagarjuna, the reason we happen to be conscious and have the body that we do and why there is a world is because the relevant causes and conditions have come together. It is not for any other reason, as many others have suggested. For example, some people have said that the world is produced from some kind of metaphysical substance, from a primary cause that does not have consciousness from which it evolved.

Primal Cause Argument

In ancient India, the Samkhya school[10] of thought presented this kind of notion. They represent a speculative philosophy that says everything originated from primal material stuff. According to Nagarjuna, this kind of idea does not make any sense. According to the Samkyhas, this primordial stuff exists outside the categories of all the physical entities that evolved from the original stuff since they are supposed to have a totally different nature.

For example, according to the Samkhya school and others of this kind, (like an ancient theory of some form of substantial naturalism) the primal substance is thought to be unchanging, but changes evolved from what the primal material stuff threw up, so that which was produced from it brought about change. According to these theories, this also means they believe in self-causation[11]. The primal stuff[12] causes everything else to arise from it, independent of anything else. The primal stuff does not need aid or assistance from outside itself since it is capable of producing everything itself. There is no notion of things coming into existence based on causes and conditions. All that is needed is the existence of the primal stuff and that is sufficient for the arising of everything in the cosmos.

Nagarjuna proposes that this idea is not coherent because what is unchanging in itself cannot bring about or create anything: it cannot be an agent. As soon as we start to speak about a primal material substance that is supposed to lack consciousness, to begin with, it would not be able to exercise will. Therefore, even if the primal material had some energy or something to produce or capacity to create something, this would automatically mean change had been introduced into the very nature of that primal substance. To "create" means the concept of time has to be present so there is a time when the primal stuff has not created something and there is a time when the primal stuff *has* created something. It is not a one-off thing but a series of actions performed by the primal stuff, so there is a time A, a time B, and a time C at which the primal stuff has been acting. Therefore, this means this primal stuff is not permanent but impermanent.

When the primal stuff is involved in these kinds of activities, then it is involved with time and it therefore becomes part of the created world and cannot then have the autonomy they claim it has. The whole notion in this argument suggests that everything is dependent on primal stuff but the primal stuff itself is not dependent on anything. As stated earlier, this philosophical position is problematic, as what is unchanging in itself cannot be a source of creation and therefore, is an incorrect view.

Theistic Argument

There are others who are theists, such as the Nyaya[13] for example, who were another ancient Indian school of thought. They believe in God, Ishvara[14] and that he creates everything. Ishvara, unlike the primal stuff, actually has consciousness and divine willpower and so forth. Ishvara also wills the world to come into existence. The Nyayikas[15] believe that the consciousness of different living creatures, different species of animals, and the whole cosmos is created by this being. They ascribe or attribute complete autonomy to this divinity, because this god is not dependent on anybody else, not dependent on anything else. Ishvara has the capacity to will anything into existence and no limitation in his divine power.

Nagarjuna says there are several problems with this position; one of which is that if the divine power, if unlimited, would be able to bring anything into existence or create anything. But that is not the case in terms of our own experience. The other point to think about is the divine being and his will. Again, as with most theists, the Nyayikas also want to believe that divine *unchangingness* is one of the special attributes of being divine. Everything else changes, everything else goes through change, but divinity does not.

So the question is posed: "Are God and his will identical or separate?" If they are identical, Nagarjuna says, this means when God wills the world to come into existence: for example, when Ishvara wills this world to come into existence, the willpower is exercised at a specific time. There is a timeframe involved in his creative exercise[16]. What this then means is the divine nature cannot be unchanging. To clarify, as God's will is identical with his nature, when his will is exercised it is exercised in a particular timeframe, so therefore God's nature is not unchanging after all.

Additionally, it is not true that his will and his nature are separate: God in himself remains totally unperturbed but his will, on the other hand, being active, then participates in worldly events and so therefore, his will initiates certain things into coming into effect. In which case, Nagarjuna says that far from God's nature being independent, it is not because God's nature is dependent on his will. Without will, God is impotent and since his will and nature are separate according to the Nyayikas, this undesirable consequence is exposed, where one would have to say that God's nature has to rely on God's will for the creative activities to be successful.

So according to Buddhism, we cannot have the right view if we are thinking about something along the lines of some kind of substantial naturalism, where some kind of primal material stuff is the source of everything that has come into existence or that there is some kind of divine agent involved in the creation and the subsequent, continual, perpetual existence of the world.

No Cause Argument

Nagarjuna proposes that the last view we should learn to discard is the view of "no cause," meaning that there is no rhyme or reason for why the universe exists in the way it does. This view does not explain anything because we do observe some kind of regularity in the world. There is some sense in which the world operates in a semi-orderly manner and not everything is random. This means that when the universe came into existence, things did not just happen in a haphazard, random fashion. If this were the case, we should see some sign of that now. From what we observe currently with regard to how the world operates and behaves, we should be able to infer that the world actually came into existence in a very haphazard, disorderly fashion but there is no indication of that. As a matter of fact, the world is governed by some form of regularity and therefore, there is no reason to think that causes and conditions had nothing to do with the world coming into existence. According to Nagarjuna, all of these views are ones we should learn to put aside, although we should not do this prematurely. We should think about these arguments and meditate on them and see whether these alternative explanations make sense or not. It is important to consider whether the explanations proposed by each school are sound. How sound is the theistic explanation? How sound is the theory of naturalism? How sound is the idea of nihilism that there is no rhyme or reason and there is no cause, and so on and so forth?

Nagarjuna states that as part of vipashyana practice we should then reflect on what the Buddhist answers to these questions are. Although prior to answering these questions some further attendant points need to be clarified.

The Three Fetters

Know the three fetters to samsara
And obstacles to self liberation
Are fixations on: morality and asceticism;
A mistaken view of selfhood; and harboring excessive doubt.

Nagarjuna says that when we think about these points we should not think that they are just philosophical exercises of no practical value. People have engaged in all kinds of distorted moral and ascetic practices due to the kinds of wrong views that have been discussed so far. We should not underestimate the importance of the sort of world view that is informing what we do and how we conduct ourselves. Some people who have fallen under the influence of what are called "*tsul trim tul zhuk chog dzin*" (*tshul khrims brtul zhugs mchog 'dzin*) in Tibetan, or "*shila vatta para marissa*" in Sanskrit, (under the influence of wrongful notions or ideas) have been led to engage in all kinds of ascetic practices. Those who hold these views engage in extreme physical torture and penance or they may engage in violence and justify those behaviors in the name of religion or spiritual practice. One may be thinking that whatever one is doing is justified by some higher authority or higher order of the universe.

Our path to liberation will be blocked if we happen to fall into these traps. Not only that, sometimes these kinds of moralistic teachings, instead of helping us develop a better sense of ourselves, can actually intensify and concretize our distorted view of the self. This is called "*satkagadrsti*" (*satkayadrsti*) in Sanskrit, or "*jig tsok la ta wa*" (*'jig tshogs la lta ba*) in Tibetan. Satkagadrsti means that when so much focus is put on these beliefs, one begins to develop a very distorted view of the self. We get lost in that way. The third fetter Nagarjuna refers to in the previous verse is skeptical doubt. In this instance this means excessive forms of doubt: not just having some doubts or questions that might arise in one's mind but doubting everything. We may doubt fundamental things, such as questioning whether there is any such thing as morality, for example, or doubting that doing harmful things is harmful. Extreme nihilistic views are part of such doubt.

Those three, namely the distorted focus on one's self, distorted forms of moral and ascetic practices, and extreme skeptical doubt, block our way to enlightenment and liberation. As we can see, distorted religious views may impact on the notion of the self and moral and ethical practices. Along with this, the notion that there is no cause and that everything happens randomly and with no rhyme or reason for anything, inflames one's skeptical doubt. All of these mistaken views hinder us from developing the correct view or right view.

To hold the right view, we first have to think about what would help us maintain the right view.

The Four-Fold Truth

> *Liberation from samsara depends on oneself alone.*
> *It is not achieved via others or through divine intervention*
> *But by cultivating an understanding of the four noble truths,*
> *Accumulating knowledge, ethical conduct, and meditative concentration.*

Nagarjuna says that in order to hold the right view, first we must understand that to achieve liberation or enlightenment we must do this for ourselves. There is no outside help in the form of divine intervention. Therefore, one should think about the four noble truths. If we think about the four noble truths, we will want to keep everything in proper perspective and maintain the right view. We would be thinking about the dissatisfactory nature of the samsaric condition, which is the first truth, and we would also know that ignorance, craving, and grasping brings about suffering and dissatisfaction in our lives. This is the cause of suffering or the second truth. When we see this, we realize that due to ignorance, which is to do with one's mind, one has the capacity to step out of that state of ignorance. It is possible for one to put an end to suffering and attain nirvana, which is the third noble truth. In order to attain nirvana, we need to embark on the path leading out of suffering and be transported to nirvana, which is the fourth noble truth. In order to do this, first one should try to broaden one's knowledge. One should try to inform one's mind about spiritual practices and other things that are of importance. One should follow the wholesome way of life. We should cultivate meditative concentration and develop wisdom based on that. Doing these things will help us to maintain the view. According to Nagarjuna, in order to stay motivated one needs to think about the preciousness of our body and so on. We should pay attention to our body and practice mindfulness of body. This is an important part of the practice.

Encouragement In The Disciplines of Ethics, Wisdom, and Concentration

> *Be disciplined in the highest ethical conduct,*
> *Highest wisdom, and highest concentration.*
> *Greater than one hundred and fifty monastic disciplines*
> *Are certainly included in these three.*

As explained previously, if we train in this way and do these practices, then the hundred and fifty disciplines—meaning even the vows that monks and nuns are supposed to keep are included in this. Nagarjuna says we should pay attention to our body because we will become more disciplined. If we do this when we are walking, lying down, standing up, sitting down or doing some kind of meditation in action, then this will also help us utilize our mind more effectively when we are doing shamatha or vipashyana meditation. As has been explained by the Buddha in the sutras, if we can pay attention to our body, the way we move about, and what we do, we will become more adept at using our mind to our advantage. Physical tension or tightness in the body and things of that kind do not help the mind. Through a more conscientious attitude towards the body and with proper handling, one could work with the body and from that gain suppleness of the mind as well.

According to Nagarjuna, the practices of mindfulness and awareness are essential components of all the Buddhist practices—from the practice of generosity to the practices of shamatha and vipashyana. If we do not practice mindfulness and awareness when we go about our normal business in everyday life, even if we have good intention, it is very hard to implement. If we do not really try to cultivate mindfulness and awareness properly, our meditation will not flourish. Sometimes if we do meditation in action and practice mindfulness, this could serve as a bridge between active meditation and passive meditation. It will help not only with the meditation practice of concentration, but also with the meditation of contemplation and reflection, such as vipashyana meditation. This is an important thing.

As part of paying attention to our body we also have to become inspired to stay alert and this is done by contemplating on how precious time is and that there is no real time to be wasted.

Impermanence and the Preciousness of Life

> *Life is plagued by vulnerabilities*
> *As water bubbles exposed to the wind.*
> *For one to inhale after exhaling*
> *And to awaken from sleep is a cherished gift.*

Nagarjuna says we should contemplate the preciousness of time and the fragility of life so that we are able to stay more focused. We will then be more effective and motivated in how we utilize our time. The best way to motivate ourselves is to understand the preciousness of time and of the opportunities we have. Anything can happen to us because of impermanence. It is like a bubble that is exploded by a gust of wind. We cannot take comfort in the thought that we will have time to get to the things we want to do, which we keep postponing and putting off. Nagarjuna states that this is not to make us discouraged, but to do the opposite: to make us act, and not get too distracted—that is the whole purpose of thinking in this way. This kind of awareness should come when we pay attention to our body, as everything is subject to change and anything and everything can happen to us.

If we do not take opportunities when they are there, we may miss out. There may not be a second time. In any case, reflecting on points like this with a sense of urgency will help us wake up and take stock of things. There is nothing else that can really motivate us as much as thinking about the shortness of time. We can try to motivate ourselves in terms of thinking about the importance and significance of what we are doing but thinking about our mortality and the limited time allotted to us in this life is the most effective way of preventing us from falling into complacency, laziness, or distraction and the diffusion of mind and activities. Therefore, it is important to think, "I have what we call a precious human body now and while I have it I should be making use of it. I will use this body to cross the ocean of samsara and through that arrive at the other shore, nirvana." These are the kinds of reflections one needs to do.

This last verse marks the end of this section of the text. The next section is devoted to the nirvana aspect, regarding what to do and how to approach and attain nirvana.

Consider the Excellent Qualities of Nirvana and Practice the Path Resulting in Nirvana

Practice the Path with Urgency

As if extinguishing a fire
That caught onto your clothes or hair
Strive to end the cycle of rebirth renouncing samsaric deeds
With urgency, there is no greater aim than this.

In this verse, Nagarjuna states he will first explain how to aim towards nirvana in a general kind of way. This way of explanation is common to the two vehicles of Buddhism; the first which is called the Small Vehicle and the second the Great Vehicle. This particular verse pertains to the teachings of both these vehicles. After we have thought about the preciousness of the human body due to the ever-present danger of losing it, we try to aim towards nirvanic liberation. Nagarjuna says when we think about nirvana we should think about it with a sense of urgency. We should think that our ordinary experience of extreme heat generated by conflicting emotions is very intense, something like fire that we should really try to put out. Nagarjuna uses the following example to elaborate this point: if a person's garments catch fire, the individual would try to put it out. In this same way, if one's hair catches fire, then immediately one would try to put that fire out. In other words, one would not stand idly by and do nothing about it. In a similar kind of way, we should think of nirvana as being a state of peace and samsara as being a very uncomfortable and unpleasant state to be in. In order to put an end to this suffering, we have to think about not interminably taking series of rebirths. We have to think in terms of putting an end to the series of birth, death, and rebirth, birth, death, and rebirth repeated eternally over and over.

According to Nagarjuna, if we contemplate the following points discussed in the next verse, we will be able to put an end to this cycle of death and rebirth.

The Three Higher Trainings

Through moral precepts, wisdom, and meditative concentration
Secure the peaceful and untainted state of Nirvana—
Ageless, deathless, inexhaustible—
A state unaffected by earth, water, fire, air, sun, and moon.

As has been discussed, the most important practices we can do in Buddhism are the three trainings: training in moral precepts, training in meditative concentration, and training in wisdom. If we train in these three, we can put an end to the possibility of having to take rebirth again and again. To attain nirvana means that we will be relieved of the suffering of old age, the suffering of death, and so on. As Nagarjuna says, the state of peace of nirvana is not something that can be perturbed by even great catastrophic collisions caused by the five elements of earth, water, fire, wind, and space and planetary upsets such as changes caused by the sun and moon and so on and so forth. To train in the three trainings properly, one should practice what is known as the "*Seven Limb*" application that is orientated towards the attainment of enlightenment or nirvana.

The Seven Limbs

> *Seven limbs to generate enlightenment—mindfulness,*
> *Discriminating awareness, vigor, joy, purification,*
> *Meditative concentration, and equanimity*
> *Accumulate virtuous conditions to create the cause for*
> *Nirvana to arise.*

To attain nirvana, we need to accumulate both merit and wisdom. If we practice the seven applications, we will be able to accomplish both these accumulations. This means that through the accumulation of merit, we can enjoy our temporary, mundane experiences in a much more fulfilling way and through the accumulation of wisdom, we are able to purify our mind so that we attain liberation and enter nirvana.

- The first limb is the practice of mindfulness. The use of mindfulness will allow us to stay focused on everything that we are doing, both physically and mentally. Mindfulness in this context is not only about being aware of whatever is present, but it denotes the capacity of the mind to be used in such a way that all the things one needs to retain, not let go of and forget, are retained. Through the use of mindfulness, one is able to retain all the virtues that one has been able to accumulate and not let them go to waste.
- One should then apply discriminating awareness or prajna in order to understand things better in terms of both their general characteristics and specific characteristics through

the practice of vipashyana meditation. The limb of discriminating awareness or prajna is needed because in order to attain this level of realization, one has to have sufficient understanding of one's own nature and the nature of reality to be able to extricate oneself from distorted views.

- Then one should practice or generate "*virya*," zestful effort or vigor. This means if one finds what one is doing to be enjoyable, then one feels energized and if one does not enjoy what one is doing, one does not feel energized. Nagarjuna states that we need the limb of vigor because to attain enlightenment or nirvana is like being on a journey, one is always moving. Development or progress does not occur in a stationary way; one has to move towards enlightenment. What propels one to go forward is dependent upon vigor.
- When we are practicing, either in terms of following our way of life, as is explained in this text, or when one is practicing the different types of meditation, it is very important to learn to take pleasure in what one is doing. Nagarjuna suggests one can teach oneself to like something. Even if one does not like doing something at the beginning, it is possible to teach oneself to enjoy something that one should enjoy, just as much as one can learn not to take pleasure in things one should not overindulge in. Joy is an important part of this because if one experiences joy, then one is inspired to do more of what one needs to do and to have more experiences of what one needs to experience in order to attain enlightenment. Joy is also an important component of the application of the enlightened factors to attain nirvana.
- The next limb concerns working with the body-mind complex. This means to try to exercise the mind so the

mind can stay alert and not become lethargic. Physically doing certain things like breathing exercises, receiving massages, doing some level of physical exercise, and watching the intake of one's food can also make the body light. In other words, heaviness in the body and heaviness in the mind make the whole psychophysical system unconducive to self-cultivation either in terms of behavioral modifications, or changes, or in terms of the transformation of one's mental outlook. "*Shin jyang*" (*shin sbyangs*), in Tibetan is the processing of the body-mind complex. This is important because when the body and mind are not workable we leave ourselves open to the afflictions of conflicting emotions. Lightness of the body and alertness of the mind make it so much easier to do all the things that have been mentioned, such as practicing mindfulness, applying vigor, or using discriminating awareness.

- The limb of meditative concentration is important because unless the mind is stable, even if not consistently or continuously, unless one has some experience of stability of the mind from time to time, it is very difficult to overcome the conflicting emotions or develop discriminating awareness. Even to develop discriminating awareness, one needs a mind that is not too fickle. When one is thinking, one has to be able to think in a deliberate fashion. If our mind is totally scattered, then we will not be able to do vipashyana meditation. Some level of concentration is needed with all these practices. This is another application that is important in this context in order to attain the *path of seeing*.
- The last limb of the seven-limb application consists of trying to develop some notion of equanimity. This means

> trying to cultivate a mind that is neither too active, where there are too many things going on in one's mind, nor a mind that has become so slow and dense that there is no sense of clarity and one is always feeling a bit drowsy or sleepy. The attainment of equanimity is important because when our mind is not churned up too much and has a sense of being quite spacious, then one is able to allow various things to occur without tipping the balance. In other words, if some disturbing thought arises, then one does not immediately become disturbed. There is an accommodating attitude that is not corrupted by excessive thinking or dullness of the mind. By using these seven limbs of application one makes one's way towards enlightenment. These seven limbs are extremely important as part of one's practice, but in Buddhism the most important form of practice is still the practice of shamatha and vipashyana: the meditations of tranquility and insight.

If we apply these seven applications, we will be able to ensure that we can successfully accomplish the two accumulations: the accumulation of merit and the accumulation of wisdom. Nagarjuna says that if we really pay attention to the application of these seven factors we will attain the first level of spiritual realization, which is called the *path of seeing*, because in order to attain the stage of the *path of seeing* we need the application or use of mindfulness, which has the function of retaining all those things that one needs to retain in oneself.

The Two Accumulations

> *Without wisdom there is no meditation,*
> *Without meditation there is no wisdom.*
> *When one has both of these the ocean of existence is held*
> *Barely, like water in a cow's hoof-print.*

In this verse, Nagarjuna emphasizes that the practitioner must practice both wisdom and concentration, as these are the most important practices one should engage in. Shamatha practice will help us to develop samadhi or meditative concentration, and vipashyana meditation will allow us to develop insight or discriminating awareness. Nagarjuna states that these practices complement each other as shamatha without vipashyana is incomplete and conversely, vipashyana without shamatha is incomplete. We should not think shamatha is one form of meditation and vipashyana a completely separate method. Doing vipashyana could in fact also help one stabilize the mind. If one develops a greater understanding of what is going on in the mind, it may also be more receptive to the shamatha meditative state. Conversely, if one can settle the mind through shamatha meditation and then engage in vipashyana meditational exercises in that state of calmness, then one may develop some insight by discriminating awareness.

Discriminating awareness is used in order to establish the right view and discard erroneous views. Therefore, we should not just do shamatha or just do vipashyana. If we just do shamatha meditation, even if we do it for a long time, we may initially think that our mind has become much calmer and things are getting better, but in the long run the conflicting emotions have not really been dealt with. They will reassert themselves. So in this way, discriminating awareness is extremely important and can be developed only through vipashyana. If one simply pursues shamatha meditation, one may be progressing with the practices and may even be able to attain the various states of samadhi that have been discussed. The four stages of meditative concentration and so on may be attained, but one does not attain liberation or enlightenment through that effort. Without developing discriminating awareness, one will not free oneself from samsaric bondage. Therefore, these two methods of meditation must be conjoined and as a result, all the other practices will become easier to do by engaging in these.

Nagarjuna states that the next important point is to develop the correct view. This is connected to the previous discussion concerning the overcoming of wrong view in terms of the naturalistic or theistic explanations, or of the nihilistic explanation of things coming into being from nothing or from no cause.

The Importance of Avoiding Speculation

> *Fourteen metaphysical pronouncements declared*
> *Unexplainable through speculation*
> *Bring disquiet to the mind*
> *So leave speculating upon them alone.*

We first have to go back to the Buddha's original discourses if we are to think about how to develop wisdom in consideration of what has so far been discussed. The development of wisdom has not been covered a great deal in the text, apart from the sorts of erroneous views that are to be discarded in order to develop the correct view. In the original discourse concerning the development of wisdom, the Buddha refused to answer certain metaphysical questions. Nagarjuna states that the Buddha showed tremendous reluctance to encourage speculative thought and this is important to understand. As far as the Buddha was concerned, one has to speculate to some extent but too much metaphysical speculation does not lead anywhere. Therefore, when he was approached and asked several metaphysical questions, Buddha refused to answer them and chose to remain silent.

Different commentators have said a number of things concerning the reason that Buddha did not answer. From Nagarjuna's point of view, the main reason was because the individuals who were posing these questions to the Buddha would have misunderstood if the Buddha had given any kind of answer. These individuals were seeking a yes or no answer, but with some of the questions it was not possible for the Buddha to respond in this way. This does not mean there was no answer at all, but rather it would not have been appropriate for the Buddha to say either yes or no. The questions that were asked of the Buddha were the following:

> Does the world have a beginning or an end?
> Are consciousness and the physical body the same or different?
> Is the self permanent or impermanent?
> What happens to the Buddha after attaining nirvana—does he continue to exist in some form or does nirvana represent some form of extinction and with post-nirvanic existence?

Nagarjuna says we can draw a couple of lessons from the choice the Buddha made not to respond to these questions. One is to realize that somebody who understands dependent arising does not need to be querulous and adopt a very clear position on these things saying, for example, that the body and mind are the same or not the same. Somebody who understands dependent arising is at peace so does not need to speak about these things. One can afford to be silent.

The other lesson that can be learned from the Buddha's silence on these questions is that too much speculation is not useful. What is relevant to us is that the reason the Buddha did not give a yes or no answer is because Buddha understood dependent arising. As the Buddha said on a number of occasions in his discourses, the most important thing that he could teach others was the notion of dependent arising. Apart from dependent arising there is nothing else. From the Buddhist point of view, everything comes into being because of interdependent arising so that body and mind, world and self—everything arises because of dependent arising. As Nagarjuna has said in another text, "*The Precious Rosary*[17]," the Buddha remained silent about the beginning and end questions. The Buddha refused to give answers to these questions because he understood dependent arising and could not explain this to his interlocutors. If Buddha had said yes or no they would not have been satisfied. Being metaphysicians, they would have wanted the Buddha to accept either one or the other horns of the dilemma, to grab hold of one or the other of these horns. If he didn't do that but instead gave a sermon on dependent arising, this would not have satisfied them, so Buddha chose to remain silent. For example, if Buddha had said that mind and body are interdependent and arise because of interdependent arising, these people would not have been satisfied with that answer. They would have wanted to know whether he really thought the mind and body were separate or identical. Therefore, Buddha saw the futility of these kinds of speculative discussions.

The Buddha's main objective was to find a way to free our minds of all kinds of mental torment. He realized that many of these speculative ways of thinking only inflame the already agitated mind more. Therefore, the Buddha did not encourage excessive speculation about varieties of metaphysical issues. Nevertheless, some kinds of speculation are inevitable. As human beings, we initially have only a limited capacity to understand things. Our potential to understand things is much greater than we are capable of at the beginning but even so, when we engage in some form of speculation this has to have direct bearing on things that immediately concern us. From the Buddhist point of view, understanding that things arise in relation to interdependent arising is the main thing. This is true both in terms of one's own organism, one's sense of self, and in relation to the external world. What sorts of beings we are and how we fit into the world have to be understood based on the notion of interdependent arising. Interdependent arising may not be something that we can immediately appreciate and understand and so therefore, it has a speculative dimension to it. Nevertheless, it is not all metaphysical:

what we say about interdependent arising does relate directly to our own psychophysical embodiments.

The Buddha's real position is referred to in the following verse:

The Twelve Links of Interdependent Arising

> The Sage declared: "From ignorance originate
> predispositions;
> From the latter, consciousness; from consciousness
> originate name and form;
> From name and form originate the six sense organs;
> From the six sense organs, contact.
>
> From contact originates feeling;
> From the foundation of feeling originates craving;
> From craving, grasping; from grasping originates
> becoming;
> From becoming, birth occurs.
>
> If there is birth, then a very great heap
> Of suffering ensues, such as sorrow, disease, old age,
> Frustration, fear of death, et cetera;
> However, by putting an end to birth, all these will cease."

In this way, the Buddha states that rather than thinking too much about whether the body and mind are separate or the same, we should be concerned about how we have come into being, how we are operating and existing now, and what is in store for us. So this is how we should think about the twelve links of interdependent arising. For example, ignorance is what causes us to engage in all kinds of physical, verbal, and mental activities. These activities are initiated by consciousness and this consciousness does not roam about in a non-attached and disembodied way. It is attached to a body, so therefore, there is a body-mind complex, which is called name and form. Name refers to consciousness and form refers to the body. When there is a body, that body comes with sensory capacities so can see things, hear things, smell things, and so forth. With the senses comes feeling, which is the next one. When the body comes in contact with things that are hot or pleasant, the body feels those experiences and when it comes in contact with something cold or unpleasant, one feels that and so on. Feeling comes from having contact because unless there is contact between the physical and what it comes in contact with, there is no feeling. So, the link of contact must be present.

When there is feeling, craving develops because whenever one finds something to be pleasurable then one craves for that. Craving leads to the perpetuation of one's existential condition. The existential condition leads to the taking on of rebirth and then when we are born into this world and endowed with all these capacities, we have the capacity to suffer. We experience myriad forms of suffering because of the kinds of beings we are. We have the senses, we have feelings and these feelings generate other kinds of propensities, predilections, dispositions, and so forth. Once we are born we are going to age. That is the natural progression. We are also going to die so death is the terminal point of our life.

The Buddha said that by thinking about the "twelve links" or *twelve nidanas* (Skt.) in this way we must think about the pain of this, because if we do not have any understanding of the way in which the self arises, there is no way of escape. If we accept the notion that there is a future rebirth in store for us, there is added reason why we should try to stop the cycle. Through understanding the twelve nidanas we can gain a better understanding of how everything about us operates as a network of interlocking, psychical, physical, and dispositional systems. This is what we should try to understand. Therefore, one is not just one thing, as there are many levels and elements operating with each other in a harmonious fashion keeping us alive. From the Buddhist point of view, we try to understand how we happen to be here with the aid of the teachings of twelve nidanas and other contemplations of this nature, these help us to see that we are not simply placed or dropped or planted here as a discrete thing. One is a complex system. Therefore, the world one inhabits is also equally complex in the sense that it is also not to be understood in any way that suggests the world came into existence from one single source, whether that single source is posited as primal material stuff or a supra-conscious being.

As Nagarjuna says,

> *This doctrine of Interdependent Origination encompasses all existence*
> *It is a profound precious treasure within the Buddha's teachings.*
> *One who sees the intricacy of Interdependent Origination*
> *Sees the excellence of the Buddha, the Knower of Reality.*

One needs to understand the teaching of interdependent origination as it relates not just to the ways things are for us as human beings, but in relation to the world itself. In Buddhism we use the notion of interdependent arising to understand and gain insight into the world. As the Buddha himself repeatedly stated, the notion of interdependent arising may seem simple, but it is not simple; it is very profound. If we really understand interdependent arising, then it makes it difficult for us to still cling onto the notion that there is self. When we think about ourselves, we cannot think there is something called the self without thinking in terms of the sense faculties, the feelings, dispositions, consciousness, the body, or in terms of the world. With this understanding, it is very difficult to say that the world is caused by primal material stuff or a supra-conscious being or that it has come into being without any rhyme or reason or cause, or that it has come into being from nothingness.

If we think of everything in terms of interdependent arising, then we can dispense with these ideas. We do not have to think about them to make sense of the world or relate to the world. In fact, the world itself displays a tremendous level of complexity. It has many different layers and elements and all these different elements do not operate individually and independently of each other, but on many different levels. There is a network of interconnecting and interlocking events, processes, and systems in place. By thinking in this way, it will help one to understand interdependent arising and by understanding, one will then be able to have the right view. One has to be guided by the right view and we will then be on track. As Nagarjuna mentioned in the previous section, wrong view means that even if we are trying to do something beneficial, it does not bear fruit or there is a diminished return from our deeds.

The next verse suggests that another way to understand what we need to do to attain nirvana is in relation to the noble eightfold path of the Aryas. Nagarjuna states that one should use the eightfold path to cross the ocean of samsara.

The Eightfold Path

> *In order to attain peace, practice these eight parts of the path:*
> *Right view, right livelihood, right effort,*
> *Right mindfulness, right meditation,*
> *Right speech, right action, and right thought.*

(1) The first one refers to the right view that has already been discussed. Adopting the right view is extremely important.

(2) The next one is right livelihood. Right livelihood refers to how to live well and manage our lives so that while leading a normal life, we still try to cultivate ourselves.

(3) Right effort means exerting ourselves and not allowing laziness to overwhelm us.

(4) Right mindfulness.
(5) Right meditative concentration.
(6) Right speech means not slandering or gossiping behind people's backs, particularly in a vicious way.
(7) Right action means not taking life unnecessarily without justification, not stealing and things like that.
(8) Right understanding comes from understanding the four noble truths.

By practicing the noble eightfold path, one can make progress with what one is doing and arrive at the other shore, the shore of nirvana. Nagarjuna says we will attain the next stage beyond the "path of seeing," which is termed the "path of meditation," by practicing all the methods that have so far been discussed. When the noble eightfold path has become actualized, we have attained the "path of meditation" and that is the next level of realization on the way to enlightenment. At the beginning, right through from the "path of seeing," we need to apply ourselves. We are guided by the notion of the noble eightfold path, which taken individually, is right speech, right livelihood, right mindfulness, right meditative concentration, and when all these things become realized within oneself one does not then need to practice them as such. One embodies and possesses these qualities quite naturally.

Nagarjuna says:

(1) Right view helps the individual to properly maintain meditative equilibrium. As mentioned before, if one has the right view, this allows the meditative practices to flourish.
(2) Right understanding helps one to help others. When one has attained right understanding, this helps one to care for others with that understanding. In this instance, how one supports and cares for others is through helping

others understand things better by bringing about a change in their outlook on life and on their situation.

(3) Right speech also helps one help others but, in this context, one helps others through verbal persuasion or verbal intercourse so that the individual can gain confidence in the things one should have confidence in. That is another way in which one helps others. In this context, we are not just talking about ordinary speech. Somebody who has attained this level of realization would be able to use speech in a much more effective manner in terms of how to instill the right kinds of values or convictions or whatever that individual needs.

(4) Right action at this level of realization means that one would be able to help others transform themselves in relation to their behavior. If one is faltering and is on a self-destructive path, then such an individual might be able to reverse the whole situation. One might be able to help others to adopt behaviors that are beneficial rather than harmful.

(5) Right livelihood is realized in terms of not having the tendency to indulge in a livelihood that is contrary to the promotion of one's wellbeing and the wellbeing of others. So that a livelihood that does not bring direct harm to anyone is attained.

(6) Through realization of right effort, all of the things that one needs to work with have now been worked with and processed. One does not need to try to find the energy or motivation to do whatever that one needs to do.

(7) Right mindfulness is also attained at this level where the disturbances caused by the secondary forms of negative emotions have subsided so one is much more easily able

to maintain a meditative way of being. One is not given to excessive proliferation of thoughts or depression, feeling down, or feeling sluggish.

(8) Right concentration or right samadhi is attained when one has been able to effectively dispel many of the delusory forms of thought. When the mind has cleared, it is like a fog has lifted and there is a sharpness to the mind that one has not experienced before.

In that way, the noble eightfold path is realized at the level of the path of meditation because one has been following the instructions given in the early part of this text.

The Four Noble Truths

From birth there is suffering;
Craving is the source and regenerator of the same;
Its cessation is through attainment of liberation;
The path to that attainment is the Noble Eightfold Path.

Always seek to realize the Four Noble Truths.
For everyone, dwelling in the lap of this richness
Crosses an ocean of defilements through attaining this knowledge,
To reside in the lap of the Buddha

According to Nagarjuna, the reason we practice Buddhism is because we want to cross the ocean of samsara and to understand the four noble truths. By understanding the four noble truths and practicing the noble eightfold path as the means to free ourselves from the first two truths and to attain the third truth, which is the Truth of Cessation or nirvana, then one practices the noble eightfold path, which is the fourth truth. All the practices we do and all the teachings that we try to understand in Buddhism, boil down to the understanding of the four noble truths. All the teachings of Buddhism have to do with understanding that life as we experience it, is full of dissatisfaction and the cause of that dissatisfaction has to do with ignorance and craving. Nevertheless, our life does not have to be like that: an end can be put to suffering through practice. We follow the various practices of right mindfulness, right livelihood, generosity, moral precepts, patience, right meditative concentration, and the cultivation of insight and all of the methods mentioned that consist of the practice of the noble eightfold path.

The noble eightfold path can be reduced to what are called the Three Trainings: training in ethics, training in meditative concentration, and training in wisdom. The various members of the noble eightfold path are grouped into those three different forms of training. Right livelihood and right action and so on are part of the training in ethics, and right mindfulness and right concentration are part of the training in meditative concentration. Right understanding and right view are part of the training in discriminating awareness or wisdom. By practicing the noble eightfold path in this way and trying to individually cultivate each one of them, one develops as an individual and begins to progress on the path. One is then able to leave this shore of samsara and arrive at the shore of nirvana. According to Nagarjuna, if one practices in this way, even if one does not leave the householder's life or is leading a normal life and has the responsibilities of a business, it is still as though one is sitting in the lap of a Buddha. Such a person would be able to cross the ocean of samsara.

Nagarjuna says to the king:

> You, yourself, being a person of many responsibilities while still remaining in the position of ruler, can practice all of these things. Even in this capacity you would be able to cross the ocean of samsara and ford the turbulent waters of conflicting emotions. So please do it in this way.

Nagarjuna says,

> *Realizers of the Truth*
> *Neither fell out of the sky*
> *Nor sprang from the earth like grain.*
> *They were formerly an ordinary person subject to defilements.*

Nagarjuna explains to the king that each person starts from the same level. People like the Buddha did not just spring up from nowhere or drop from the sky or something of that nature. Buddha and people like him were ordinary beings with lots of defilements. What we need to understand is that these people had the same problems and experiences that we ourselves have. Instead of thinking that they were completely different kinds of people entirely, we should think that if they could attain enlightenment and do it through understanding the four noble truths, then we could do the same. Nagarjuna says that if one has proper teachings and guidance, then that is all that is necessary, given that one is willing to apply oneself on the path.

Disciplining the Mind Toward Virtue

> *Fearless King, the Buddha has said*
> *The mind is the root of all—virtue and non-virtue,*
> *good and bad.*
> *So you must discipline the mind to virtuosity always.*
> *This heartfelt advice I give you is beneficial.*
> *No more than this need said.*

In this verse, Nagarjuna is saying that what he has said in his Letter has come from his heart. Whatever he has said is said through pure intention, with the intention to benefit and help the king. It is his hope that the king will hold this in his mind and apply himself accordingly. The Buddha has said that the mind is the root of everything, both good and ill. If we put the mind to good use, a successful outcome is guaranteed. There is nothing else that we need: it is just that we have not done this in the past, so we should start with that.

Maintain Persistence in Applying the Methods

It is difficult even for a monastic in isolation
To follow the advice being given to you.
Yet one's life will be meaningful through cultivating
The essence of these contemplations and practices.

Nagarjuna states that he is in full cognizance that what he is suggesting the king do is a great deal. He acknowledges that even an ordained person, such as a monk or nun, would find it extremely difficult. The point is that one has to do whatever one can and not doing anything at all is the root of all our downfalls. As long as we are doing whatever we can, given our limitations, then that is the most important thing. Whatever practices we can do we should try to do. The king must do the same thing. As already explained, if we do something and do it often enough, there is nothing that does not become easier. Our capacity is extended through sheer practice. If we do something over and over then through familiarity, whatever the task might be, it becomes easier and this is what the king needs to realize as well. It might be very difficult for the king to do all the practices perfectly or to his satisfaction, but nevertheless, he should do whatever he can with whatever practices he can do. If done on a regular basis, as often as possible and if the king tries to habituate himself to the practices and methods, then they will become part of his own makeup, of his way of being.

The Fruition of The Path

Rejoicing in the virtues of all living beings
And dedicating this benefit to all.
The threefold good conduct you engage in
Accumulates for the attainment of Buddhahood for all,

Mastering the whole yogic path
Fortunate will be for countless births
In the realms of gods and people
Through accumulating an abundance of merit.

According to Nagarjuna, if the king perseveres and continues on this path, he will go from strength to strength and will not only manage to free himself from samsaric entanglements, but will be of tremendous help to many others who feel defeated and wearied and beaten down. Since the king has been able to pacify his mind, he will become like the Buddha Amitabha[18], the Buddha Amitayus[19]. There would be no difference between the king and Amitabha, as it is said here.

Born as Arya Avalokitesvara[20]*, his enlightened activity aiding the stricken,*
Dispels disease, the suffering of old age, and minds full of grasping and aversion,
Dwells for limitless lifetimes in Protection of the world,
The Blessed One, Amitabha, within this Buddha-field.

The king will be of tremendous help by being able to overcome old age, sickness, and so forth.

Having exceeded the attainments of the exalted realms, sky bound and on earth
Your exceptional qualities, unblemished fame
Through attaining wisdom, virtue, and generosity
Can subdue the desires of the exalted and the ordinary
And all seekers of excess.

Having gained the qualities of the Buddha, by extinguishing fear
One can benefit multitudes of living beings afflicted by defilements,

Through attainment of the faultless, ageless, and fearless state
Peaceful, transcendent and beyond description.

According to Nagarjuna, if we engage in the practices he has been instructing the king to do, we will find them to be beneficial not only in terms of one's spiritual progress, but even as a normal person. Even ordinary people would be tremendously impressed or would think that such a person who has these qualities and conducts their life in the manner described would be somebody that everyone would look up to. These are not the kinds of qualities that people denigrate and say are worthless. Similarly, if one develops these qualities, then one would even be able to exceed the attainment of the gods and goddesses of the god realms because a truly developed human being is matchless: a fully-fledged, fully evolved, fully realized human being. Such a being would be able to outshine even the extra-terrestrial beings or the gods of other realms. Even though it may be said that such a being has transcended the world in terms of their attainment, at the same time, such a being may not abandon the world. Such a being would not have the fear of being harmed by being in the world. If such a person still had fear of being harmfully affected by the world, then all the practices would not have been of great help. While the enlightened being's mind is not governed by our normal conceptions of various things in terms of what one needs to do or achieve and accomplish, an enlightened being quite naturally through their own nature continues to benefit those in need and put others on the pathway out of suffering.

Concluding Remarks

This concludes this particular text known as "*Suhrillekha*." As discussed, this is a very, very important text and it is one that Tibetan Buddhists of all schools study. In Buddhism, we do many different kinds of practices and receive many different kinds of teachings. A text like this puts it all together and gives us an overall picture so we can see where everything fits in and what the interrelationships are between these diverse elements.

Lamp on the Path of Enlightenment by Atisha[21] is a similar kind of text. If we study these kinds of texts and continue to study and practice teachings of Mahamudra[22], they complement each other very well. Mahamudra teachings may not refer to these kinds of teachings, but this is not because they are not important. One should know and be practicing teachings like these already. We should understand and think about these kinds of practices and then study and do the Mahamudra type of meditation. We should not think it's an either/or kind of thing and that there is an option. There is no real option. We have to study and practice these things and then supplement them with Mahamudra practice and not the other way around.

In other words, we can't bypass these practices if we are serious about Buddhism. We should be practicing in this manner and if we want to go further, we can practice Mahamudra or other forms of teachings. This is the traditional view and I'm sure it is the correct one. As mentioned previously, sometimes people do a lot of meditation and they may even do meditation for quite a number of years and then get discouraged because they think they are making little progress. This could happen if one is only doing meditation and there is no real overall sense of what one is doing in one's life. As Nagarjuna says, it is important to put it all into perspective and have the correct view. This means we have to truly hold the dharmic view in order to follow the dharmic path. We don't need to have any kind of resistance to what is called "right view." To put in effort to develop the right view, we don't have to necessarily demonize and denigrate other views. There is a fine balance between being able to distinguish what is called the noble view from ignoble views but at the same time to not see other views as being completely wrong or distorted. For whatever it's worth, this is at least my view. This is how Buddhism is taught and I think it's an important way to look at it. The right view is the middle view in Buddhism. This gives a very big leeway. Right view is not a narrow view and middle view is not a narrow view. Narrow views are the extreme views and middle view is supposed to avoid extreme views. To adopt the middle view is a flexible space to be in. It's not confining or restrictive. That's the Buddhist view, at least the way I understand it.

Notes

1. A concise history of Nagarjuna is included in the introduction of this book. In brief, Nagarjuna is considered one of the most important scholars of Mahayana Buddhism tradition by most and considered a great philosopher within Asian history generally.

2. *King Gautamiputra* was the king of Andhra in the South India and was Nagarjuna's patron and friend.

3. There are four major schools in Tibetan Buddhism: *Nyingma*, *Kagyu*, *Sakya*, and *Gelug*. The Nyingma School is known as the oldest school of the four. The Kagyu school is sometimes referred to as the practice lineage with its emphasis on meditational practices. The Sakya tradition developed during the second period of translation of Buddhist scripture from Sanskrit into Tibetan in the late 11th century. The Gelug school is the newest of the four schools and has a general emphasis on study and scholarship.

4. *Mahayana* (*theg pa chen po*) is often translated literally as "great vehicle." This phase of Buddhism arose several hundred years after the Buddha. The practice of Mahayana is not determined by doctrine, school, or belief systems, but by the internal attitude held by the practitioner. That is, the attitude to seek to benefit and work for others on the spiritual path, by so doing one also benefits but one is not the central focus. Benefitting others is seen as the central motivation for seeking enlightenment but one does not seek to remain in nirvana but rather remains for the benefit of all beings.

5. *Arya* is a Sanskrit word that means elevated, precious, or pure and is used in Buddhist texts to indicate the person being

referred to is seen as exceptional, a spiritual warrior.

6. *Moral precepts* (*sila*, *tshul khrims*) are considered guidelines rather than moral laws of conduct. These are categorized into 5 guidelines of conduct: abstaining from harming sentient beings, the environment and so forth; abstaining from taking what is not given through coercion or other deceptive means; abstaining from sexual misconduct or harmful sexual activity; abstaining from false and idle speech such as gossip or character assassination; abstaining from excessive use of alcohol and other intoxicants. The purpose of practicing the moral precepts (and taking on specific precepts for a short or extended time) is three fold: to practice restraint from harmful activities; to generate wholesomeness through engaging in positive activities; and to develop skilfulness when seeking to benefit other sentient beings.

7. *The six paramitas* or transcendental actions are practices used to reduce and relieve our suffering. They are the practice of: generosity, patience, moral precepts (see above in note 6), vigor, meditative concentration, and wisdom. The development of a spontaneous and open mind is seen as the basis for the growth of a fundamental sense of generosity. Generosity can be expressed materially, through seeking to give without expectations of a return; through seeking to protect those who are vulnerable; and through the skillfully imparting the Dharma. Patience is seen as the antidote to anger, frustration, resentment, hostility, and the like. One can actively work on patience to provide a more positive and unconditional inner environment. Vigor points to the importance of applying enthusiasm, energy, and maintaining motivation on one's spiritual journey to progress the immediate goal of self improvement, and the ultimate goal of enlightenment. The development of meditative concentration is seen as key to

developing self understanding and thus progressing on the spiritual path. When meditation is practiced skillfully, one develops both wisdom and compassion. Wisdom provides insight into the sentient, and more specifically the human condition as well as the nature of reality. Here when we speak of reality, it refers to the insubstantial and transient nature of all things, and the interdependence of all things. So it is proposed that when we investigate the mind through insight or analytical meditations, we are able to refine our understanding of how the mind works and how we relate to the world as samsaric beings. The samsaric tendency is to see things as, or desire things to be, static or at least self-serving. That is, serve our comfort and desire for happiness. Recognizing the cycle nature of "desire for" and "dissatisfaction with" our experiences sets up an ongoing cycle of grasping and fixation. Thus by observing how the mind works and what compels us to seek happiness leads to an ongoing state of dissatisfaction and suffering. Insight into these habitual compulsions and their causes is considered part of the process of gaining wisdom into the tendency we have to perpetuate samsara. As these realizations deepen, from a Mahayana perspective, one seeks to not only free oneself from this samsaric bondage but first seeks to free others from this bondage. Ones spiritual journey focuses on the desire to reach enlightenment for the benefit of all sentient beings. The development of compassion provides an opportunity to act in the world with this wisdom and understanding in a way that can benefit others. Both the development of wisdom (insight into the nature of reality, and sentient and the human condition) and compassion (the act of seeking to provide what ever is essential to assist other beings) is seen as the greatest outcome from a practitioner's point of view. So training in the six paramitas provides the opportunity to develop essential qualities on the Mahayana path to reduce one's immediate suffering and increase one's ability to benefit sentient beings.

8. *Divine abode* or divine mind refers to refined mental states that can be attained through the practice of meditative concentration and our psychological attitude. Such training also includes the practice of the six paramitas (see note 7) to refine both our conduct, meditative equipoise, and insights.
9. *Bodhicaryavatara* often translated as "A Guide to the Bodhisattva's Way of Life," is a text written by Shantideva who was an 8th century Indian Buddhist monk and scholar. Bodhisattva, in the title of the text refers to a practitioner who seeks to delay passing into nirvana due to their compassion for sentient beings and their desire to help those who are suffering.
10. *Samkhya* school is an ancient Indian school that believed that the world consisted of two main realities, *purusa* (consciousness), and *prakrti* (matter). They do not believe in an all powerful God but rather that both purusa and prakrti are required to come together for something new to arise or manifest in the world. Purusa is seen as unlimited and prakrti can have qualities that are both physical and non-physical. For example, both the body and mind are considered to fall under the category of Prakrti. Prakrti has a primal nature. Things come into being, and physical events occur due to prakrti. These primal causes or substances suggest a sense of permanency or fundamental permanent nature. The aspect of permanency is in contrast to the Buddhist view of insubstantiality and emptiness. That is, that things have the ability to arise, change and dissipate due to their impermanent insubstantial nature.

11. *Self Causation* is also often referred to as self-organization. The theory of self causation in brief suggests that things emerge and change due to low-level components that by nature are the cause to propel self preservation, self generation, and self improvement and that these changes are self-regulated. This theory suggests that external causes and conditions are not necessarily required for things to change, arise, and dissipate but there is a pre-existing low level primal components that by nature is interactive and self propelling. This is not referring to a consciousness but rather a fundamental property of a living being. This fundamental property then provides the opportunity for a person to make conscious decisions and develop different abilities. So patterns or systems emerge locally and globally from numerous interactions among these low level components and their biotic activities. In this theory the quality of the choices and decisions we make are not necessarily shaped by the low level causations but are propelled by them.

12. *Primal matter* consists of two fundamental components of physical matter and the soul or mind stream. These two components are seen as having enduring qualities and the ability to morph. Further from note 10, Prakrti for example, can be described within the Samkhya belief system as primal matter. Prakrti has an enduring primal permanent aspect to its nature.

13. *Nyaya* is one of the major schools of Hinduism in India. It literally means method or judgment. This school's most significant contributions to Indian philosophy was systematic development of the theory of logic, methodology, and its treatises on epistemology. This school shares some of its foundation methodology such as the cause of suffering with Buddhism. A key difference between the two is the Nayaikas (followers of the Nyaya religion) believe in the existence of an

enduring soul, and the unchanging nature of God. Where as Buddhism is non-theistic and has a central foundation of impermanence and insubstantiality within its doctrine.

14. *Ishvara* is the omnipotent God within the Nyaya religion. Believed to be male, Ishvara is believed to have created the cosmos and can will anything into existence. In some respects Ishvara has some similar qualities to the Christian God.
15. *Nyayikas* are followers of the Nyaya religion (see notes 13 and 14).
16. In this instance God or Ishvara is referred to as "he" as in Hindu mythology/belief Ishvara is depicted as male.
17. In the *Precious Rosary* also known as the "Rosary of Precious Stones" (Ratnavali) Nagarjuna offers advice on how to conduct our lives without excessive speculation on that which will not serve to enhance us. Speculating on such matters as the beginning and end of the world can disturb the mind rather than elevate it. However contemplating interdependence can bring more clarity, humility and openness to the mind thus freeing up the mind from unhelpful conceptual disturbances and assisting in the accumulation of wisdom.
18. *Amitabha* is known as the Buddha of infinite light. In Tantric or Vajrayana practices Amitabha is seen as a deity of longevity (extension of ones life in order to continue to practice the Dharma to walk the path to enlightenment). Amitabha is the form body or nirmanakaya of longevity. Iconographically appears in the form of the Buddha.
19. *Amitayus*, similar to Amitabha is also a deity of longevity (see note 18). Amitayus, is the apparitional or sambhogakaya form of longevity. Iconographically Amitayus appears in the form of a Bodhisattva (highly realized being who instead of passing

into nirvana remains to benefit beings). Amitayus is often presented as one of a trio of longevity deities along with White Tara (female Buddha) and Ushnisha Vijaya (female deity used in tantric practices).

20. *Arya Avalokitesvara* is the diety of compassion and is iconographically depicted as a Bodhisattva. In Tibetan Avalokitesvara is known as *Chenrezig*. It is a commonly held that His Holiness the Dalai Lama is the physical manifestation of Chenrezig.

21. The text *Lamp on the Path of Enlightenment* by Atisha sets out the Buddhist path within the framework of three levels of motivation on the part of the practitioner: the Hinayana (self realization), Mahayana (self realization for the sake of others) and Vajrayana (self transformation) paths. Atisha's text became the source of the lam rim tradition practiced predominantly by the Gelug school of Tibetan Buddhism but is also practiced by all schools in Tibetan Buddhism. It is also know as the graduated path to enlightenment. Atisha was an Indian Buddhist scholar and yogi from the 11th Century.

22. The Mahamudra approach to meditation practice is uniquely designed to lead to ultimate realization by revealing the nature of the self and reality. The Mahamudra practices and contemplations are not done with the use of such ritual processes as deity visualization, recitation of mantras and so forth. However Mahamudra practice can be done alongside sutric and tantric practices. These practices and contemplations helps reveal our many preciously held beliefs and fixations lack intrinsic reality and that our misconceptions, and view of reality, and the world are sustained by habitual thought processes and our responses (of aversion, attraction or neutrality) to our sensory intake.

Bibliography

Introduction

"Collection of Reasoning." *Lotsawa House*. Accessed March 10, 2018. www.lotsawahouse.org/tibetan-masters/khenpo-namdrol-tsering/madhyamakavatara-1.

Della Santina, P. (n.d) *Nagarjuna: A Good Friend*. A Buddhist Library. Accessed March 10, 2018.
http://www.abuddhistlibrary.com/Buddhism/A%20-%20Tibetan%20Buddhism/Authors/Nagarjuna/Nagarjuna%20-%20A%20Good%20Friend/friend.htm

Gyalwang Karmapa's Teachings on Nagarjuna's "Letter to A Friend"—Detailed Report. Karmapa—*The Official Website of the 17th Karmapa, 2009*. Accessed March 10, 2018.
kagyuoffice.org/gyalwang-karmapas-teachings-on-nagarjunas-letter-to-a-friend-detailed-report/

Kaluphahana D. 1986. *Nagarjuna The Philosophy Of The Middle Way*. Albany, State University Of New York Press.

Lopez, Donald S. "Nagarjuna." *Encyclopaedia Britannica*. August 23, 2017. Accessed March 5, 2018.
https://www.britannica.com/biography/Nagarjuna.

Padmakara Translation Group. 2005. *Nagarjuna's Letter to a Friend*. New York. Snow Lion Publications

Westerhoff J. 2009. *Nagarjuna's Madhyamaka*. New York.

Oxford University Press.

Main Text

The text referred to by Traleg Rinpoche was a 2004 reprint:
Jamspal, L, Chopel, Ngawang S., Santina, Peter D. *Nagarjuna's Letter to King Gautamiputra*, Motilal Banarsidass, Delhi.

Glossary

Aryadeva: (third century). A scholar of the Indian Madhyamaka school and a direct student of Nagarjuna, he is best known for the text *Catusataka* (Four Hundred Verses).

Awareness: (*jneya, shes bzhin*). The process of being alert and perspicacious. This type of awareness is spontaneously generated in meditation practice as the principle means of accessing the innate wisdom consciousness.

Bodhicitta: (*byang chub kyi sems*). Literally "enlightened heart," this is something we can only generate by thinking about the welfare of others in the cultivation of wisdom and compassion.

Bodhisattva: (*byang chub sems dpa'*). Literally an "awakening being" who has committed themselves to the path of compassion and the practice of the six paramitas while dedicating their actions to the welfare of all beings (See also transcendental perfections).

Buddha: (*sangs rgyas*). Someone who has eliminated emotional and cognitive obscurations and achieved full enlightenment.

Compassion: (*karuna, snying rje*). The wish that other beings may be free from suffering and the cause of suffering. It is materialized through the transcendental perfections of generosity, moral precepts, patience, and vigor and is the cause of leading an effective and fulfilling life.

Conditioned existence: (*samsara, 'khor ba*). The vicious cycle of transmigratory existence, which arises out of ignorance and is characterized by suffering.

Conflicting emotions: (*klesha, nyong mongs*). The emotional properties that dull the mind and cause us to misapprehend the true nature of existence.

Dependent Origination: (*pratityasamutpada, rten 'brel*). Everything exists in dependence upon everything else, which means that nothing has an autonomous existence in its own right, but has simply come into existence due to causes and conditions.

Excessive Desire: (*raga, 'dod chags*). A craving for the objects of the senses that gives rise to grasping and fixation because excessive desire is always intensified rather than ameliorated by acquiring the object of desire.

Dharma: (*chos*). The whole body of the Buddha's teachings.

Discriminating awareness: (*prajna, shes rab*). This is an immediate experience of genuine, penetrating, intuitive insight, which cannot be conveyed in intellectual terms. It is the ability to discern things very clearly without being perturbed by the whimsical moods that allow the disruptive influence of our impulses and delusions to overwhelm us.

Eight worldly dharmas: (*asta lokadharmah, 'jig rten chos brgyad*). In this context dharmas mean "factors," so there are eight worldly factors or four pairs of factors. These are loss and gain, pleasure and pain, praise and blame, and defamation and fame.

Emptiness: (*sunyata, stong pa nyid*). The understanding that persons, phenomena, and conceptual frameworks are devoid of any inherent existence and therefore nothing more than mere appearances.

Enlightened One: (*sangs rgyas*). Buddha has managed to rid himself of all confusions, conflicting emotions and debilitating tendencies (*sangs*) and to cultivate all the positive qualities of awakening (*rgyas*).

Enlightenment: (*bodhi, byang chub*). Literally "the awakened state," it comes to completion with the development of compassion and the commitment to skillful means in order to liberate all sentient beings. The final fruition of complete liberation transcends all duality and conceptualization.

Equanimity: (*upeksa, mnyam bzhag*). A spacious state of mind that is free from attraction, aversion, and indifference.

Five faculties: (*pancendriya, dbang po lnga*). These include trust, vigor, mindfulness, meditative concentration, wisdom and are called "faculties" (*driya, dbang po*) at the beginning of the bodhisattva path and "powers" (*bala, stobs*) when the bodhisattva has made some real progress on that path.

Five aggregates: (*panca-skandha, phung po lnga*). The self is a collection of aggregates or psychophysical constituents. No single aggregate can be identified as the self; we simply have a notion of a self when all these aggregates come together. The five aggregates are the physical body (*rupa-skandha, gzugs kyi phung po*), feelings (*vedana-skandha, tshor ba'i phung po*), habitual dispositions (*samskara-skandha, 'du byed kyi phung po*), consciousness (*vijnana-skandha, rnam shes kyi phung po*), and perceptual experience (*samjna-skandha, 'du shes kyi phung po*).

Four Immeasurables: (*caturaprameya, tshad med bzhi*): immeasurable love (*maitri, byams pa*), is the wish for all sentient beings to meet with pleasure and the cause of pleasure; immeasurable compassion (*karuna, snying rje*), is the wish for all sentient beings to be free from suffering and the cause of suffering; immeasurable joy (*mudita, dga' ba*), is to celebrate others fortunate situations. This comes from seeing all sentient beings as having the capacity for happiness and the cause of happiness and having the potential to be free from suffering and the cause of suffering; and immeasurable equanimity (*upeksa, btang snyoms*) is stability of mind that has the ability to generate a very positive feeling toward all the different kinds of sentient beings, situations and circumstances.

Four meditative concentrations: (*chatur-samadhi, bsam gtan bzhi*). The four stages of samadhi attained through shamatha meditation, where we gradually attain meditative experiences leading up to the experience of one-pointed concentration and then a deep state of meditative absorption. Each state is said to correspond to the states of the gods or elevated states of one consciousness.

Four Noble Truths: (*chaturarya-satya, 'phags pa'i bden pa bzhi*): the Truth of Suffering (*duhkha-satya, sdug bsngal gyi bden pa*), the Truth of the Cause [of suffering] (*samudaya-satya, kun 'byung gi bden pa*), the Truth of Cessation [of suffering] *(nirodha-satya, 'gog pa'i bden pa*) and the Truth of the Path (*marga-satya, lam gyi bden pa*) that transports us to nirvana.

Generosity: (*dana, sbyin pa*). This is one of the six transcendental actions as well as one of the six recollections, because learning to be generous is regarded as the very foundation of our ethical practices. It also makes the cultivation of all other virtues and perfections much easier.

Gods: (*deva, lha*). The gods reference is associated with mental cultivation, because the elevated and divine states of existence are analogous to the deepening levels of absorption associated meditative concentration.

Ignorance: (*moha, gti mug*). An erroneous way of understanding, based on a lack of awareness where we go about our business in a mindless and inattentive fashion without being fully conscious of what we are feeling, thinking, and doing and thereby attributing an existence to beings and things that is solid, real, independent and inherently existing.

Impermanence: (*anitya, mi rtag pa*). This is the idea that the transient nature of everything is the fundamental property of every conditioned thing. This fact is the basis of life because without it, existence would not be possible.

Insight meditation: (*vipashyana, lhag mthong*). The cultivation of wisdom by gaining a insight into how the mind substantializes everything through distorted thinking and imputing fictitious characteristics and attributes to things.

Intention: (*abhipraya, dgongs pa*). For a specific action to be fully karmically weighted, it has to be accompanied by the motivation or intention to carry out that specific act, because the intention is what makes it a deliberate act.

Karma (*las*): Literally "action," this is the unerring law of cause and effect, where positive actions bring happiness and negative actions bring suffering.

King Gautamiputra: (1st-2nd century A.D.). He was the historical Andhran king who ruled in Central India during Nagarjuna's lifetime and who was the recipient of Nagarjuna's letter.

Liberation: (*moksa, tharpa*). This is the final release from the cycle of death and rebirth and all the suffering and limitation of worldly existence.

Madhyamaka: (*dbu ma*). Literally "the middle way" school of Mahayana Buddhism, it was founded by Nagarjuna and Aryadeva and emphasizes the doctrine of emptiness. The middle way describes the position taken by its adherents in relation to the existence of non-existence of things. Madhyamaka uses elaborate reasoning to prove that things do not have any enduring essence.

Mahayana: (*theg pa chen po*). Literally "great vehicle," the teachings of this phase of Buddhism arose several hundred years after the Buddha's paranirvana and emphasize emptiness and compassion. They spread throughout Asia to China, Tibet, and Japan became the established form of Buddhism in those countries.

Meditative concentration: (*samadhi, ting nge 'dzin*). We refine our mental states through the practice of meditative concentration. This is one of the three trainings that are essential to Buddhist practice. However, this training is not sufficient to lead us to enlightenment, but must be combined with the training in ethical conduct, and more particularly, the training in discriminating awareness or wisdom.

Merit: (*punya, bsod nams*). The psycho-spiritual dispositional properties we need if we hope to enrich our lives, cease feeling empty and vacuous, avert obstacles, and prevent adversity.

Middle view: (*madhyam-drsti, dbu ma'i lta ba*). The understanding of Dependent Origination where we neither latch onto a metaphysical concept of the self nor deny the existence of such a concept. If we fail to hold the middle view, we might also fall into the extreme of upholding absolute reality at the expense of relative reality or visa versa.

Mindfulness: (*smrti, dran pa*). The capacity of the mind to remember what it needs to know to attain the path of seeing, because it enables the retention of the virtues we have accumulated and makes us impervious to the upsurges of disturbing states of mind. Mindfulness and awareness are essential components for all the Buddhist practices and our meditation will not flourish without it.

Moral precepts: (*sila, tshul khrims*). We should base our cultivation of moral precepts on the practice of generosity and maintain them with pure motivation and they will open the way to liberation and increase our sense of autonomy.

Nagarjuna: (1st-2nd century A.D.). One of the principle founders of Mahayana Buddhism and the Indian philosopher who founded the Madhyamaka School after he systematized and deepened the teachings of the Perfection of wisdom sutras. Arguably the most influential Indian Buddhist thinker after Gautama Buddha, he provided the most comprehensive and methodological presentation of the Buddhist notion of emptiness.

Nirvana: (*mya ngan las 'das pa*). Characterized as the cessation of suffering, nirvana is the goal of spiritual practice in Buddhism, signifying liberation from cyclic existence and the exhaustion of karma.

Noble Eightfold Path: (*aryastanga-marga, 'phags pa'i lam yan lag brgyad*). This is how we cross the ocean of conditioned existence and arrive at the other shore of nirvana. It includes right view (*samyag-drsti, yang dag pa'i lta ba*), right understanding (*samyak samkalpa, yang dag pa'i rtog pa*), right speech (*samyag-vac, yang dag pa'i ngag*), right action (*samyak-karmanta, yang dag pa'i las kyi mtha'*), right livelihood (*samyag-ajiva, yang dag pa'i 'tsho ba*), right effort (*samyag-vyayama, yang dag pa'i rtsol ba*), right mindfulness (*samyak-smrti, yang dag pa'i dran pa*), and right meditative concentration (*samyak-samadhi, yang dag pa'i ting nge 'dzin*).

Path of meditation: (*bhavana-marga, sgom lam*). The stage where we actualize the Noble Eightfold Path and no longer need to apply ourselves, because we have actualized the Noble Eightfold Path within ourselves and now embody all the necessary qualities quite naturally.

Path of seeing: (*darsana-marga, mthong lam*). The first level of spiritual realization, where we realize the Four Noble Truths within ourselves. We attain this path by applying ourselves to ethical conduct, meditation, and wisdom through mindfulness and awareness and the seven limbs of application.

Precepts: (*upavasa, bsnyan gnas*). We are doing two things when we observe precepts: restoring our wholesomeness and removing our undesirable characteristics. The precepts are similar to taking medicine, which has the dual function of eliminating illness and restoring health.

Preparation: (*samjna, 'du shes*). For a specific action to be fully karmically weighted it has to be accompanied by the intention to carry out that act and certain preparations must have been made to act.

Latent imprints: (*vasana, bag chags*). These are the predispositions and tendencies that reside in our basic consciousness.

Relative truth: (*samvrti-satya, kun rdzob bden pa*). The level of phenomenal appearances that are explained by Dependent Origination and synonymous with "how things appear."

Right view: (*samyak-drsti, yang dag pa'i lta ba*). A view that leads to liberation, by leading to a genuine and authentic understanding of our human condition, which in turn leads to discriminating awareness or wisdom.

Seven limbs of application: (*sapta-bodhyanga, byang chub yan lag bdun*). Aspects of the three trainings that accomplish the accumulations of merit and wisdom and enable us to attain the path of seeing. These are mindfulness, discriminating awareness, vigor, pleasure, restraint, concentration, and equanimity.

Shantideva: (695–743). An Indian Buddhist scholar at Nalanda

University and an adherent of the Madhyamaka philosophy, he is renowned for his Bodhicharyavatara, a verse poem about the Mahayana path to enlightenment.

Six recollections: (*sadsmrti, dran pa drug*). These are the Buddha, Dharma, Sangha, gods, generosity, and moral precepts.

Six transcendental perfections: (*sad-paramita, pha rol tu phyin pa drug*). The six perfections include generosity (*dana, sbyin pa*), moral precepts (*sila, tshul khrims*), patience (*ksanti, bzod pa*), vigor (*virya, brston 'grus*), meditative concentration (*dhyana, bsam gtan*), and wisdom (*prajna, shes rab*).

Ten non-virtuous deeds: (*dasa akusala, mi dge ba bcu*). If we wish to lead a wholesome life and attain our ideals, we need to know what actions to abandon. There are ten actions we should refrain from committing. These are killing (*prana-tighata, srog gcod pa*), stealing (*adatta-dana, ma byin par len pa*), engaging in sexual inappropriate conduct (*kama-mithya-cara, 'dod pas log par gyem pa*), lying (*mrsa-vada, rdzun du smra ba*), slander (*pai-sunya, phra ma*), causing friction between people (*parusya, tshig rtsub mo*), gossip (*abaddha-pralapa, ngag bkyal ba*), covetousness (*abhidhya, brnab sems*), the intention to harm others (*vyapada, gnod sems*), and wrong views (*mithya-drsti, log lta*).

Ten virtuous deeds: (*dasa kusala, dge ba bcu*). There are ten actions we should cultivate, which are the opposite of the ten non virtuous deeds. These are saving lives, generosity, appropriate sexual conduct, honesty, praise, mending friendships, minding our own business, rejoicing in the fortunes of others, beneficial intentions, and right view.

Three Jewels: (*tri-ratna, dkon mchog gsum*). Literally "three precious ones," these are the essential components of Buddhism: the Buddha or Enlightened One, the Dharma or teachings of the

Enlightened One, and the Sangha or members of the community who follow those teachings.

Three trainings: (*trisiksa, bslabs pa gsum*). These are the training in moral precepts (*sila, tshul khrims*), the training in meditative concentration (*samadhi, ting nge 'dzin*), and the training in wisdom (*prajna, shes rab*).

Tranquility meditation: (*shamatha, zhi gnas*). A basic meditation practice common to most schools of Buddhism, the aim of which is to tame and stabilize the mind in order to practice insight meditation.

Trust: (*sraddha, dad pa*). One of the qualities that amass the wealth of the Noble Ones and one of the five faculties/powers. It is a form of wealth because it enables us to develop rapport with the Buddha, Dharma, and Sangha, and be comfortable in the company of others. It is a power, because we need to believe certain things are workable to operate in a positive way.

Twelve Links of Dependent Origination: (*dvadasanga pratityasamutpada, rten cing 'brel bar byung ba'i tshul bcu gnyis*). These are ignorance (*avidya, ma rig pa*), mental activities (*samskara, 'du byed*), consciousness (*vijnana, rnam par shes pa*), "name and form," (*nama-rupa, ming dang gzugs*), contact (*sparsa, reg pa*), feeling (*vedana, tshor ba*), craving (*trsna, sred pa*), grasping (*upadena, nye bar len pa*), becoming (*bhava, srid pa*), birth (*jati, skye ba*), old age and death (*jara-marana, rga shi*).

Two accumulations: (*sambhava-dvaya, gnyis kyi tshogs*). The accumulation of merit (*punya-sambhava, bsod nams kyi tshogs*) determines the kind of human beings we will become by enabling us to avert obstacles and prevent adversity. We accumulate merit through the practice of generosity, moral precepts, patience, and vigor. The accumulation of wisdom (*jnana-sambhava, shes rab gyi tshogs*) is how we overcome ignorance and attain the transcendental state of awakening. We accumulate wisdom through the practices of tranquility and insight meditation.

Ultimate reality: (*paramartha, don dam*). Synonymous with emptiness, it can only be known through direct experience.

Ultimate truth: (*paramartha-satya, don dam pa'i bden pa*). There are two views of reality, one that sees things as they appear to exist (relative reality) and the other that sees things as they are (ultimate reality). The level of absolute truth refers to "how things exist."

Vinaya: One of the three sections of the Buddhist Canon, along with Sutra and Abhidharma, it contains the rules of the Buddhist order and the vows of the Buddhist monastics.

Virtues: (*dad pa*). Virtue is built on character and is intimately connected with the attainment of our ideals on the spiritual path. If we wish to lead a wholesome life and attain our spiritual ideals, we need to know which actions to cultivate and which to abandon. Nagarjuna makes a distinction between ordinary virtues on the Dharmic path and the transcendental virtues of the Mahayana path as contained in the six transcendental perfections.

Vows: (*samvara, so thar*). There are seven sets of vows within Buddhist ordination: the vows of the monk (*bhikshu, dge slong*), nun (*bhikshuni, dge slong ma*), novice monk (*sramanera, dge tshul*), novice nun (*sramanerika, dge tshul ma*), probationary nun (*siksamana, gelopma*), layman (*upasaka, dge bsnyen*), and laywoman (*upasika, dge bsnyen ma*).

Wisdom mind: (*jnana, ye shes*). An innate capacity of the mind, which gives rise to genuine insight when the obscurations of deluded consciousness are eradicated.

Wisdom: (*prajna, shes rab*). This is cultivated through concentration and insight, is the cause of direct insight into the reality of things.

Wrong view: (*asamyag-drsti, yang dag med lta ba*). If we wish to calm our minds and cultivate sound ethical qualities, our motivation will be of no help if we have the wrong views of dualism, monotheism, or nihilism. Believing that refraining from negative actions will not lead to fulfilling experiences, that there is no connection between our actions and our future experiences, that spiritual practice will free us from any obligation to act in a responsible and ethical manner are aspects of nihilism.

Index